1-Hour WordPress 2023

A visual step-by-step guide to building WordPress websites in one hour or less!

Dr. Andy Williams

https://ezseonews.com

Updated 21st February 2023

"I work in the education department at one of the top academic institutions in the U.S., and if I could hire Dr. Williams to write all of my online training, I wouldn't hesitate." Laura

What people are saying about previous versions of this book:

"I'm moderately technical but have NO (nada, none, zero) experience creating a website. I used this book to make it through my first pass. I need to build out content now, but the structure and workings of my site are set. I appreciated Dr. Williams' conversational style, that was very easy to follow and implement. Don't hesitate - get this and get to work!" **Bruno Lenni**

"Dr. Andy Williams really left nothing to be confused about and gave us EVERYTHING to build a webpage in one book! Well done, great layout, easy to follow... Finally, I have a starting point for my own webpage... (still procrastinating though!)" **Jamie**

"I'm now a webmaster!" **Leo Hayes**

"Complete, quick, and to the point. Just what most people need. Good information. No filler. Great price. A well thought out book by Dr. Andy Williams" **Zoie Brytin**

"This guide or, more accurately, a manual is an excellent training guide by a teacher that I have been learning from for many years. It is well written and laid out and will help you learn WordPress without stress. Highly recommended." **Dale Reardon**

"By following the steps in the book, you'll easily have your WordPress site up & running in no time and, as Andy knows his stuff, you can be confident it will be set up well." **SBUK**

"Great content from a great author! Highly recommended!" **David H**

"I have read articles which say just set up a WordPress blog, and I haven't the faintest idea, but this book is very simply and carefully written, so no steps are left out. Andy is an expert who seems to be able to explain things in a way which helps the non-expert. A rare talent. It gave me the confidence to have a go." **Chris Wade**

"I think everyone thinking of building a WordPress website should read this guide first. I've been using WordPress for several years, and I am amazed at how much I didn't know about WordPress. The guide takes you through the whole process of getting web hosting, buying a domain name, designing your website to help with Search Engine Optimisation, and everything else you need to know about posts versus pages, widgets, plugins, and lots more. Dr. Andy has a very pleasant writing style which concentrates on what to do and why to do it, without making lots of unnecessary remarks just to fill out a few more pages. And the bonus is that readers get access to his website, which he built alongside writing the book, and he plans to provide a lot more relevant information there in the future." **John D Bridson**

"The step by step approach is excellent." **Carole**

"Doing anything for the first time can be daunting. Putting up your first WordPress site is

no different - especially for the software challenged. Luckily this book offers an easy-to-follow step-by-step process covering all that is needed to overcome any lack of previous experience. With this guide in hand, a new site can realistically be in place in a matter of hours." **John Gergye**

"With this product, it was as if he read my mind (or was watching over my shoulder)." Alan **Northcott**

"The first thing I want to say about "Rapid WordPress Websites" is that you should download it immediately because you need to look no further for information about building your first WordPress website." **Norman Morrison**

"Dr. Andy walks you through the WordPress setup process, step by step. He explains the why's of the steps you are taking, what to do, how to do it, and why you should do it. "Rapid WordPress Websites" is a great instructional refresher guide for even the Pro." **E. W. Aldridge, Sr**

"Anyone who gets this book and follows the steps will be able to have their own website up and running in no time. I hadn't installed a WP blog in years and had forgotten how to do it. Dr. Andy's book made the process simple and painless." **J. Tanner**

"I have been struggling with my WordPress Website - not anymore. This is a must-read for beginners, and I bet even some long-time users will find information in Andy's book. I now realize how little I knew about WordPress. The great thing about this book is it walks you by the hand to get your site going and getting down to business. This is one of those books that you will refer to time and time again. So, keep it handy!" **Suzanne Dean**

DISCLAIMER AND TERMS OF USE AGREEMENT

The author and publisher of this eBook and the accompanying materials have used their best efforts in preparing this eBook. The author and publisher make no representation or warranties with respect to the accuracy, applicability, fitness, or completeness of the contents of this eBook. The information contained in this eBook is strictly for educational purposes. Therefore, if you wish to apply ideas contained in this eBook, you are taking full responsibility for your actions.

The author and publisher disclaim any warranties (express or implied), merchantability, or fitness for any particular purpose. The author and publisher shall in no event be held liable to any party for any direct, indirect, punitive, special, incidental, or other consequential damages arising directly or indirectly from any use of this material, which is provided "as is," and without warranties.

The author and publisher do not warrant the performance, effectiveness or applicability of any sites listed or linked to in this eBook.

All links are for information purposes only and are not warranted for content, accuracy or any other implied or explicit purpose.

The author and publisher of this book are not in any way associated with Google.

Table of Contents

Introduction

Firstly, thank you for buying my book.

This book teaches anybody (even complete non-techie beginners) to quickly create a website by working through the book, chapter by chapter.

I have written other books on WordPress, but this one is special. The emphasis in this one is to teach you on a need-to-know basis and not cover everything WordPress can do (my WordPress for Beginners book & course both do that).

After reading this book, if you still want more, check out my WordPress books and courses here:

https://ezseonews.com/books

https://ezseonews.com/courses

Updates & Changes to WordPress?

When this book was written, the current version of WordPress was 5.6. However, the WordPress ecosystem changes a lot, and while most of these changes will be minor (you may not even notice them), some bigger changes can happen. After this book is published, there isn't much I can do to notify you of these changes. Therefore, I have set up a page on my website for book owners so that updates, changes, and issues can be listed. If something in the book does not look right, visit the updates page here:

https://ezseonews.com/wp2023/

You can leave comments on that page if you need to.

A Note About UK v US English

There are some differences between UK and US English. While I try to be consistent, some errors may slip into my writing because I spend a lot of time corresponding with people in both the UK and the US. The line can blur.

Examples of this include the spelling of words like optimise (UK) v optimize (US).

The difference I get the most complaints about is with collective nouns. Collective nouns refer to a group of individuals, e.g., Google. In the US, collective nouns are singular, so **Google IS** a company. However, in the UK, collective nouns are usually plural, so **Google ARE** a company. This is not to be confused with Google, "the search engine," which is singular in both.

There are other differences too. I hope that if I have been inconsistent anywhere in this book, it does not detract from the value you get from it.

WordPress itself will have some differences depending on whether you are using UK or US English. The one I find most obvious is in the labeling of the area containing things you have deleted.

If you installed WordPress with US English, you'd see this called "trash":

Comments

All (1) | Pending (0) | Approved (1) | Spam (0) | Trash (0)

But if your WordPress is installed with UK English, this becomes "bin":

Comments

All (2) | Pending (0) | Approved (2) | Spam (0) | Bin (0)

There are other places in the dashboard that use localized words like this. I'll leave those for you to find.

Found Typos in This Book?

Errors can get through proof-readers, so if you do find any typos or grammatical errors in this book, I'd be very grateful if you could let me know using this email address:

typos@ezseonews.com

I will make sure these errors are corrected for the next version of the book.

What is WordPress?

WordPress is a Content Management System (CMS). That just means it is a piece of software that can help you manage and organize your content into a unique and coherent website.

WordPress was created as a blogging tool, but it has become so much more than that over the years. Today, many WordPress-driven sites look nothing like blogs (unless that's what the user wants). This is down to the flexibility of this fantastic tool.

WordPress powers simple blogs, corporate websites, and everything in between. Companies like Sony, the Wall Street Journal, Samsung, New York Times, Wired, CNN, Forbes, Reuters, and many others all use WordPress as part of their online presence.

WordPress is open source, meaning that all its code is free to view, use, and customize. Being open-source has enabled programmers worldwide to create extensions to this powerful publishing platform, from website templates to plugins that extend this brilliant site-building tool's functionality.

Some of the Features That Make WordPress Great

• The template system for site design means that changing your site's look and feel is as simple as installing a new theme with just a few clicks of the mouse. There are a plethora of free and quality WordPress themes available.

• Plugins are pieces of code that you can download into your WordPress site to add new features and functions. There are tens of thousands of plugins available, and many are free.

• Once your site is set up, you can concentrate on adding great content to your site. You simply build your page in the WordPress Dashboard, hit publish, and WordPress takes care of the rest.

• WordPress has a feature called Widgets that allows the user to drag and drop "features" into their site. For example, you could add a visitor poll to your site's sidebar using a widget. Widgets are typically used in the sidebars and footers, but some templates allow widgets to be placed in other well-chosen areas of the design.

• WordPress can help you with the SEO (Search Engine Optimization) of your site so that it has the potential to rank higher in search engines like Google and Bing.

• WordPress can create just about any type of site, for example, a hobby blog, a business site, or an e-commerce store.

WordPress.com v WordPress.org

The first thing that confuses many WordPress students is that there are two types of WordPress. These are found on two separate websites.

If you visit WordPress.com, you can sign up to create a WordPress site for free. WordPress.com hosts your site on their servers, meaning you do not need to buy a domain or hosting. The downside is that there are limitations. WordPress.com controls what you can and cannot do on your site. For example, you won't be able to customize WordPress in the way you want because you cannot just install any theme or plugin you want. You also won't be using your own domain name. Your website address will be something like this:

AndysBlog.WordPress.com

This type of domain is called a sub-domain, and it is hosted on the WordPress.com website. Therefore, you do not own the domain, and WordPress.com could theoretically close your site down if they think you are abusing their terms of service.

There are paid options on WordPress.com which allow you to use your own domain, but the price for doing so is greater than if you just use WordPress.org in the first place. Even worse, unless you are subscribed to the most expensive WordPress.com plan, there will still be restrictions.

I don't recommend WordPress.com for building sites.

WordPress.org, on the other hand, is a site where you can download the WordPress software for yourself, install it on a server of your choice, and customize it however you wish. This allows you to create a website that you own, and you can do whatever you want on it. You also get to choose your own domain name, like:

AndysBlog.com

Doesn't that look better? Be aware that domain names are on a strictly first-come, first-served basis. You obviously cannot choose a domain name that someone else already owns.

This book uses WordPress from WordPress.org. You'll be buying a domain name and building the site on a web host.

NOTE: It is possible to install WordPress on your own computer if you just want to learn without the expense of buying a domain and subscribing to a web host. That is beyond the scope of this book, but you will find tutorials on my ezseonews.com website.

Let's get started...

Domains, Registrars & Hosting

Your domain name is important to you. It will be your website address where you can send your friends & family to view your site. It is the website address that Google and other search engines will send people. Therefore, choosing a domain name is important, and you want to get it right the first time. You cannot get a refund on a purchased domain name if you find you made a spelling mistake or changed your mind about the name.

Two types of domain name

There are two main types of domain names. The first category, which I suggest you avoid, is often referred to as "Exact Match Domain," or EMD for short.

An EMD is a domain name that exactly matches a phrase you want to rank for in Google. For example, if you decide you want to be #1 on Google when anyone searches for "Healthy Coconut Oil," then an EMD would be something like:

- Healthycoconutoil.com
- Healthy-coconut-oil.com
- Healthcocounutoil.org

See how the exact phrase makes up the domain name?

This used to work well in Google, and in the past, we could easily rank sites for phrases by choosing an EMD for the phrase of interest. However, things have changed. EMDs can cause you problems, including getting your site penalized by Google or even banned if you are not careful.

I, therefore, suggest you choose my second category of domain name – a brandable name.

A brandable domain name is one that is memorable and could be used as branding. Think of Google itself. This is a brand name we all recognize, but what would have happened if they had chosen "best search engine" as an EMD? Bestsearchengine.com doesn't have the same ring to it, does it?

Why not look up the meaning of Google and see how the name was ultimately chosen for the search engine?

I recommend you sit down and think about your domain name carefully. Avoid choosing a name simply because it contains a phrase you want to rank for in Google. Instead, think of a memorable name that people will remember when they hear it.

Imagine being out and about and you see a friend. You want to send them over to look at your new website, but you don't have a pencil to write the name down. The domain name you choose should be memorable enough that your friend can remember it once you tell them.

TLDs

TLD stands for Top Level Domain and simply refers to the extension given to your domain. Possible

TLDs include .com, .org, .net, .co.uk, .de, etc. There are new TLDs coming out on a regular basis, and it can all be confusing for beginners.

Some TLDs are country-specific, e.g., **.co.uk** is used for websites targeting the UK.

My advice on choosing a TLD is simple.

If you only want to target one country with your site, choose the TLD for that country:

.es for Spain

.co.uk for the UK

.de for Germany

If your site has a global appeal, choose a .com.

How much is it all going to cost?

Since we need to buy a domain and hosting, you may already be wondering how much this is going to cost. Let me break it down for you:

You need to buy a domain, which will cost around $10 per year. You buy domains from "domain registrars" (see below).

You need to get web hosting, and that starts from around $3 per month. You buy web hosting from a "web host" (see below).

These are your only required costs, though obviously, you can decide to buy a premium WordPress theme and maybe some commercial plugins. However, these are not required, and you can build a great-looking, feature-packed site without any additional costs.

Your total essential costs for a self-hosted website will be around $46 per year. That's not bad, considering you'll be able to get your message out to the entire connected world.

What is a Domain Registrar?

A domain registrar is a company that you buy your domain name from. Good registrars will make sure your domain auto-renews at the end of the year, can keep your site "anonymous," lock your domain so it cannot be transferred to another individual without your approval, and a lot of other administrative stuff.

What is a Web host?

A web host is a company that rents out computer space to anyone that wants to create their own website. They are responsible for making sure your site is up and running 24/7. All websites can go down at times (as I am sure you have seen), but good web hosts will have your website up and running 99.9% of the time.

All-in-one registrar and web host?

When you sign up with a web host, they will offer to be your domain registrar as well. The advantage is that all the bills you receive are from the same company, meaning you only have to deal with ONE company.

There are disadvantages to this arrangement, though, and many people (including myself) prefer to keep the host and registrar separate.

Potential problem: If, for any reason, your web host decides your website is causing them problems (i.e., they get spam complaints or your website is using up too many system resources), they can take your site down without any warning. What happens next?

If you use a combined web host and registrar, it goes something like this:

1. Your site goes down.
2. You contact your host, and they tell you that they received spam complaints about your domain.
3. They refuse to put your site back up.
4. You need to move your site to a new host, but your existing web host is the registrar and can make that difficult.
5. Your site remains down for a long time while you sort things out and eventually move the site to a new host and registrar.

Time to resolve this? Weeks or months.

OK, let's see what happens if your registrar is separate from your host.

1. Your site goes down.
2. You contact your host, and they tell you that they received spam complaints from your domain.
3. They refuse to put your site back up.
4. You order hosting with a different company and copy your site to the new host.
5. You log in to your registrar account and change the name servers to the new host. This takes seconds to do.

Time to resolve this? Your site is back up within 24 hours or less on the new web host.

This is one scenario where using a separate host and registrar is important.

Another scenario, which doesn't bear thinking about, is if your hosting company goes out of business (it does happen sometimes). What becomes of your site? Well, you probably lose it AND your domain name if your hosting company is also your registrar.

If your registrar and host are two separate companies, you'd simply get hosting somewhere else and change the name servers at your registrar. With this arrangement, your site would only be down for 24 hours or less.

Another situation that I have heard about is when a hosting company locks you out of your control panel (a login area where you can administer your domain(s)) because of a dispute over something. That means you cannot possibly move the domain to a new host because you must have access to that control panel to do it. Consequently, your domain will be down for as long as the dispute takes to resolve.

A final word of caution! I have heard horror stories of people not being able to transfer their domain out from a bad web host. Even worse than that, the domain they registered at the hosting company was not registered in their name but in the name of the hosting company.

For all of the above reasons, when you are ready to buy hosting, please consider using a separate web host and registrar. I'll show you exactly how to set this up so you do not have to figure this out on your own.

However, if you just want the easy option of using one company, I'll show you how to do that as well.

Domain, Host, Registrar & Installing WordPress

There are many web hosts out there, and many have their own methods for installing WordPress. To make things worse, the installation and setup process can change, often without notice.

As I write this book, I am acutely aware of what happens when things change. Suddenly, I get a lot of emails from readers asking for help because the book is wrong. This happened in the 2020 version of the book. I created a comprehensive tutorial showing how to install WordPress on a web host, only for things to change weeks after the book was published. Thankfully I had the updates page (covered earlier), which all readers could access, so I could address those issues. However, I still got a lot of emails from readers who had forgotten about that page.

So, from the 2021 version of this book, I started to do things differently based on two facts:

1. The world of hosts and registrars can change quickly, meaning that information can quickly become out of date.

2. The installation process is very visual. I've had a lot of feedback from readers (and students on my courses) asking for a video tutorial instead of written instructions.

I decided to create a page on my site where you can access up-to-date tutorials on getting hosting, a registrar, and installing WordPress. If something changes during the year, I can update those tutorials. Therefore, you will always have up-to-date information.

You can access this page here:

https://ezseonews.com/whr

This page has links to 3 different tutorials. You only need to follow one of these tutorials based on your requirements.

1. You want to use a separate host and registrar (recommended).

2. You want to use the same company as the host and registrar.

3. You already have hosting and just need to install WordPress.

When you are ready to get started, go to this page and decide which option you want to follow.

Login and Logout of your WordPress Dashboard

The WordPress Dashboard is where you go to add content and customize the look of your site. Think of it as the control center for your website.

You should have bookmarked the URL already, but if you ever forget or lose your admin link, just add **/wp-admin/** to the end of your domain URL.

This is what the login page looks like:

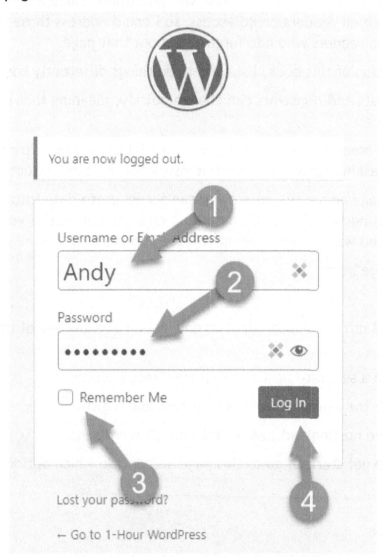

Enter your Admin username and Admin password. I recommend you check the **Remember Me** box so that it remembers your login details next time.

Now click the **Log In** button.

You will be taken inside the dashboard. Here is mine:

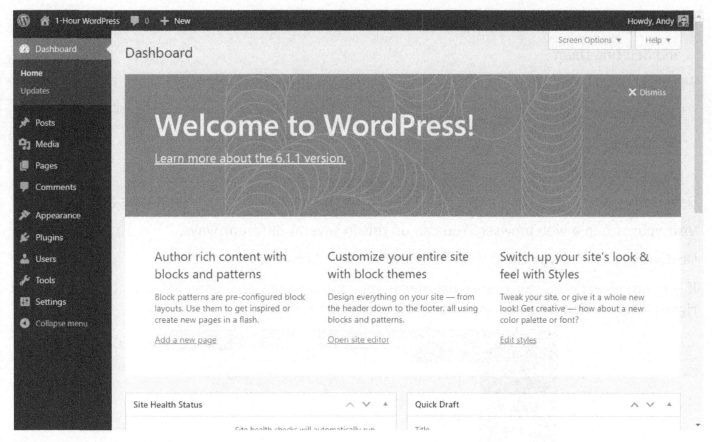

OK, this is where the fun starts.

Looking at the demo page, post, and comment

.. and deleting them

When you install WordPress, you will get some demo content installed by default. This includes:

- A post

- A page

- A comment

Don't worry about posts and pages; we will discuss them later. For now, let's take a quick look.

Visit your site in a web browser. You can do this in several different ways.

Obviously, you can type the domain URL into the web browser.

If you are already in your dashboard, move your mouse over your domain name (top left). Now right-click the **Visit Site** link and select **Open link in a new tab**.

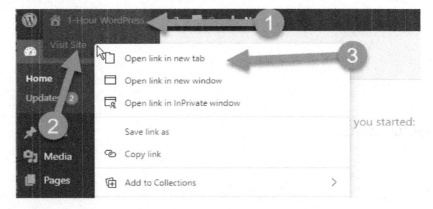

Your website will open in a new tab.

This is your homepage, and you should see a post titled "Hello World."

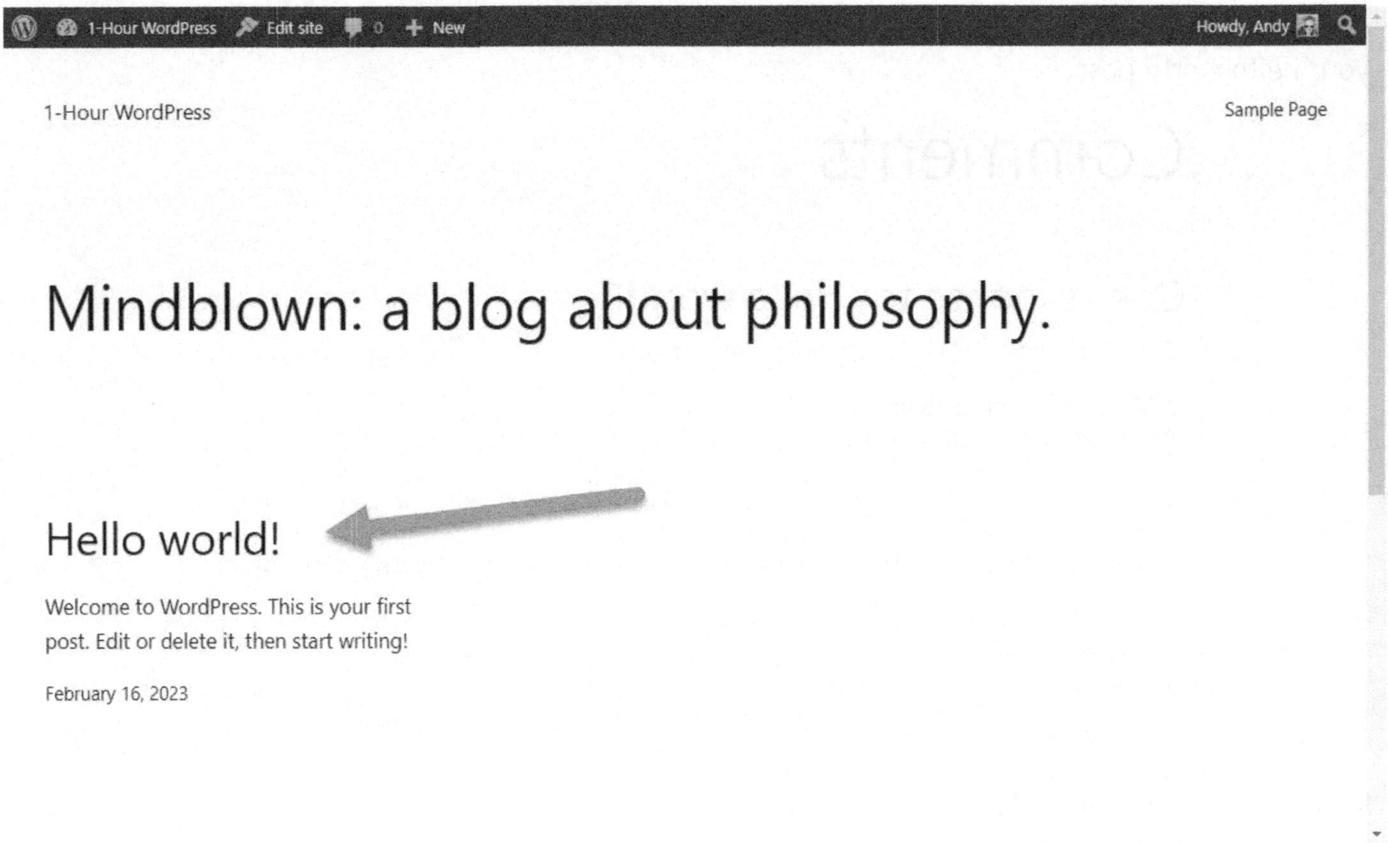

1-Hour WordPress
Edit site
New
Howdy, Andy
1-Hour WordPress
Sample Page
Mindblown: a blog about philosophy.
Hello world!
Welcome to WordPress. This is your first post. Edit or delete it, then start writing!
February 16, 2023

The style and layout of the homepage (and every other page on the site) will be determined by the theme you have active. When WordPress is installed, it is likely to use the latest theme provided by WordPress. As I write this, that theme is called Twenty Twenty-Three, and my screenshot above shows my new website with Twenty Twenty-Three active. If you have a different theme active, your homepage will look different.

A note on the homepage

The homepage is a special page. By default, WordPress will show your most recent ten posts on the homepage (there is only one on your homepage right now because there is only one post on your site - the "Hello World" post).

NOTE: Showing the last ten posts on a site is how most blogs are set up. If you are not creating a blog and you would rather have a carefully written homepage article instead, you can. Check out the section later when we look at "static" homepages.

The homepage can display the full post(s) or what is called excerpts. What it shows depends on the WordPress theme you are using and how you set it up. While the latest posts appear on the Homepage, you should also know that they also each appear on their own "post page." If you click the "Hello World!" title shown in the screenshot above, you will be taken to the post's page.

This page contains the single post in its entirety, any comments on the post, and a "Leave a Reply"

comment box for visitors to leave a comment. You'll notice that WordPress created a comment on your hello world post.

Comments

One response to "Hello world!"

 A WordPress Commenter
February 16, 2023   Edit

Hi, this is a comment.
To get started with moderating, editing, and deleting comments, please visit the Comments screen in the dashboard.
Commenter avatars come from Gravatar.

Reply

Go and have a look at your "Hello World" post.

When you installed WordPress, a "Page" was also installed. We can find that in the dashboard.

Log in to the Dashboard.

A quick way to get into the Dashboard is to use the admin bar across the top. This will appear when you are viewing your site AND already logged into the dashboard. Here it is:

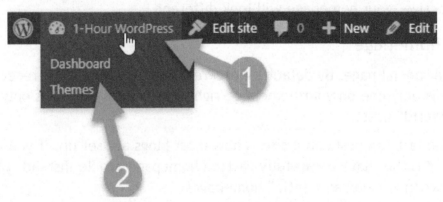

Move your mouse over the site name and click on **Dashboard** to get in.

On logging in, you'll have a menu down the left:

You can see the menu items for "Posts," "Pages," and "Comments."

Click on the Posts menu item, and you'll be taken to a screen listing all posts on the site.

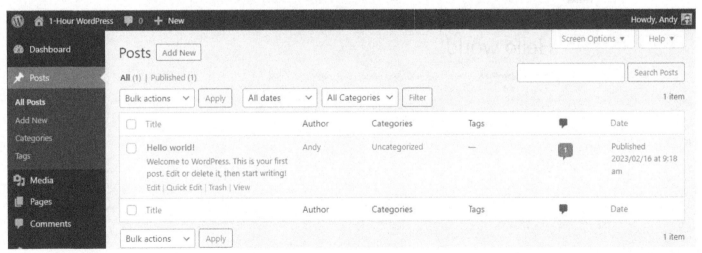

In my screenshot, I can see a short description and a menu under the title of the post. Can you? If you cannot see this, click the **Screen Options** button top right, and select **Extended View** and **Apply**.

Now, there's only one - the "Hello World" post. No surprise there, as we haven't added any yet. If you want to go in and edit the Hello World post, click on the title, and you'll be taken to the post edit screen. If you do that, click the back button on your browser when you've had a look around. OK, click on the "Comments" menu in the left sidebar.

This screen looks like the posts screen we saw previously. All the comments on the site are listed. At the moment, there is just the one that WordPress installed.

The **"In Response To"** column tells you where the comment was left. You can see that this comment was left in the Hello World post. You can click on the "Hello World" title in that table to open it in the edit post screen:

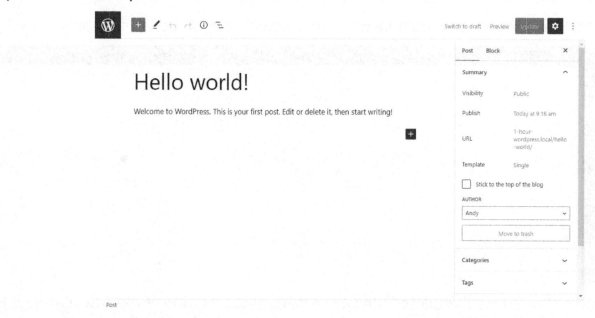

We will look at this editor later in the book. However, before we move on, did your left sidebar menu disappear? If it did, then your Gutenberg editor (the editor used to write your content) has been set as full screen. To disable full screen and show the left sidebar menu again, click on the button that has three vertical dots, and click on the **Fullscreen mode** option to deselect it:

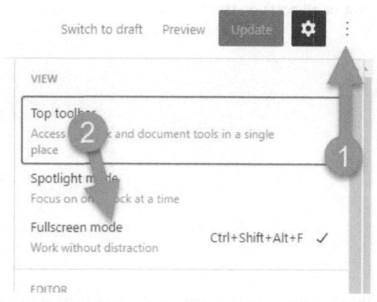

You should find the left sidebar returns:

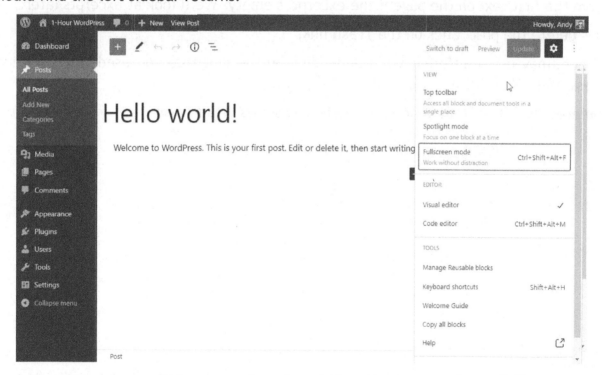

Whatever you choose here will be remembered next time. In my case above, Fullscreen mode will be disabled by default from now on.

You can click on the 3-dots button again to hide that menu 😊.

Deleting the Demo Post & Comment

To delete a post, click on **All Posts** inside the **Posts** menu in the dashboard sidebar again to return to that table showing a list of all posts on the site:

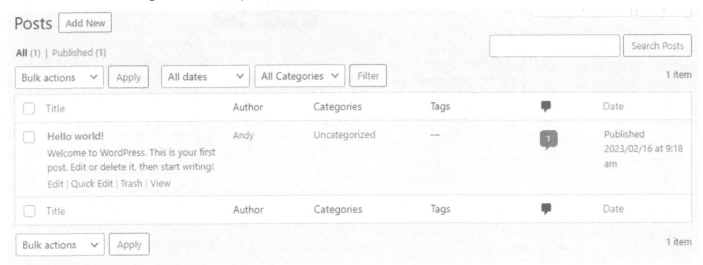

The description under the title will be taken from the **Excerpt** field of the post if it has been filled in or from the first text on the page if the excerpt is empty. We'll look at excerpts later.

OK, let's delete the post. Click on the **Trash** link.

Note: Yours may use a different word depending on the language you used when you installed WordPress. e.g., UK English installations will say **Bin**.

Once deleted, you'll see that your list of posts now shows (1) in Trash:

If you click the **Trash (1)** link, you'll open the trash:

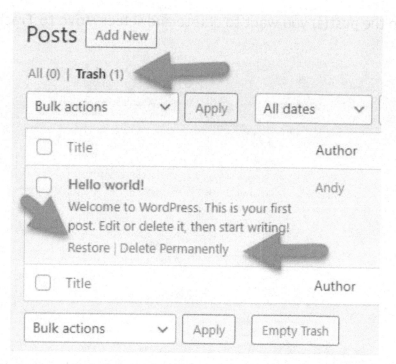

The trash contains all posts you've deleted (assuming you haven't emptied the trash), so you can see the Hello World post. The Trash acts as a safety net. If you decide you want to restore a post you've deleted, you can. Or you can delete it permanently.

There is another way to delete posts. To demonstrate this, I'll restore the Hello World post from the trash by clicking the **Restore** link.

Once restored, go back to the "All Posts" list again. There is the post, back from trash. You'll notice that the post has been unpublished and is now a draft:

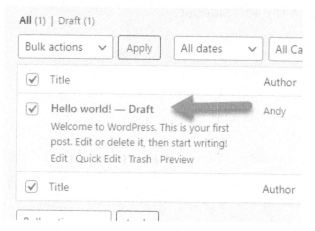

Draft posts do not show on your website. They are considered works-in-progress and will remain hidden until you publish them.

If you want to re-publish a post you have restored from the trash, just go into the edit post screen and publish as you would any other post. We'll look at publishing later.

Check the box next to the post(s) you want to delete and select **Move to Trash** from the drop-down box.

Then click the **Apply** button to move the selected posts to the trash.

This method of deleting posts is useful if you want to delete several posts. A similar system works in the comments and pages sections. You can delete comments or pages one by one, or select several and send them all to the Trash in one go.

OK, now let's look at the Pages that WordPress installed.

Deleting Demo Page

Click the **Pages** menu item in the left sidebar.

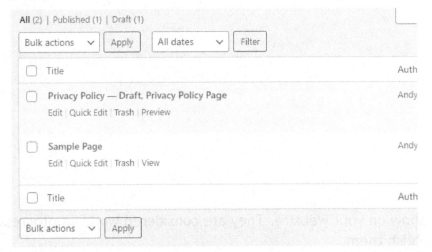

It's a familiar screen, isn't it? It's very similar to the screen for posts and for comments.

WordPress created two sample pages. One is a draft (unpublished) that you can use for a privacy policy; the other is a sample page.

Click the **Sample Page** title to open the page in the Page editor.

You'll see that the main editor window is the same as the one for posts, though other options on this screen are different. We'll look at those later. Click the back button on your browser to go back to the "all pages" list.

Delete the sample page in the same way you deleted the "Hello World!" post. The page will go to the page trash, which you can go into if you need to restore a page.

OK, we've deleted the post, which also deleted the comment associated with the post. We've also deleted the page. Therefore, the site is now pretty empty. There may still be a bit of stuff that your theme is adding, which you can see in the screenshot below:

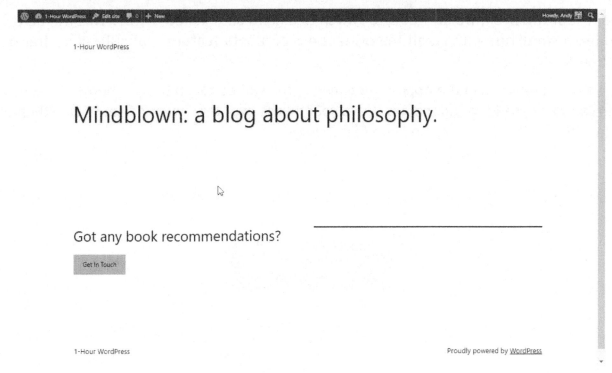

This Twenty Twenty-Three theme adds a heading plus a question about book recommendations. Weird! Not all themes will do that.

The Twenty Twenty-Three theme is a special kind of theme called a **Full Site Editor** theme. I'll cover FSE briefly in an appendix at the end of this book, but we won't be going into detail as it is not a beginner topic, and it is still in beta. If you look at the **Appearance** menu on the left, you'll see that the editor is labeled as such:

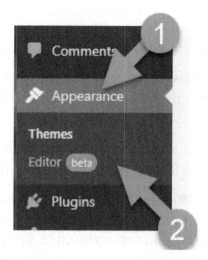

For the rest of this book, we are going to switch to a non-FSE-enabled theme. This will be the best way to learn WordPress without all the distractions of a beta feature that still, quite frankly, has a lot of bugs.

Click on the **Themes** link in the **Appearance** menu. You will be taken to the **Themes** screen, where you can see some pre-installed themes. Move your mouse over the Twenty Twenty-One theme. This is the last of the WordPress-created non-FSE themes.

Click the **Activate** button.

Now have a look at the Appearance menu:

A number of items have been added.

Customize, widgets, menus, background, and theme file editor. All of these items were not available in this menu when the FSE-enabled theme was active because the Full Site Editor handles all of these things.

By working with a non-FSE-enabled theme, we can learn how to handle these components in a much more user-friendly way so that the transition to FSE at some point in the future makes a lot more sense.

With the Twenty Twenty-One theme active, go and visit your site. You'll see that this theme has changed the appearance of your site dramatically. That is what themes do. If you scroll to the bottom of the homepage, you'll see several "widgets":

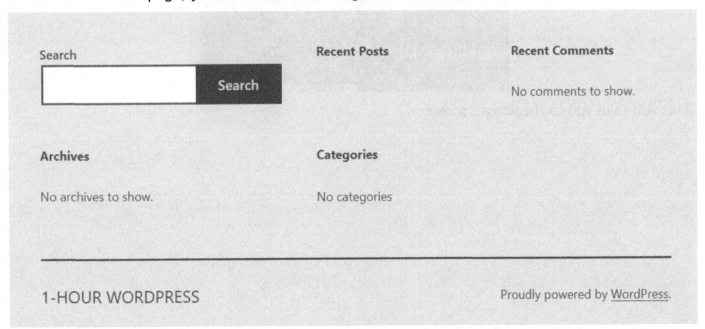

We didn't see these at the bottom of the webpage when the Twenty Twenty-Three theme was active. Let's clear them out.

Deleting Widgets

A widget is simply a "feature" that you can add to your website in predefined areas of the page, e.g., the sidebar, footer, etc.

The previous screenshot showed several installed in the footer area of the website under the Twenty Twenty-One theme. We see:

- A search box widget.

- A recent posts widget.

- A recent comments widget.

- An Archives widget.

- A Category widget.

Let's explore the widgetized areas, then delete those widgets.

In your Dashboard, move your mouse over the **Appearance** menu, and click on **Widgets**:

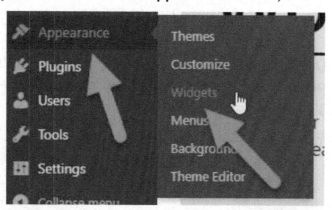

This will take you to the widget screen:

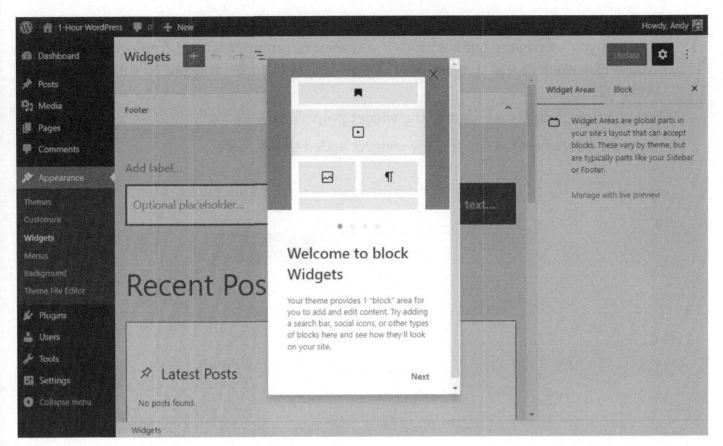

The first time you go there, you'll probably see the popup help. Read through this if you want, but when done, click the X to close it.

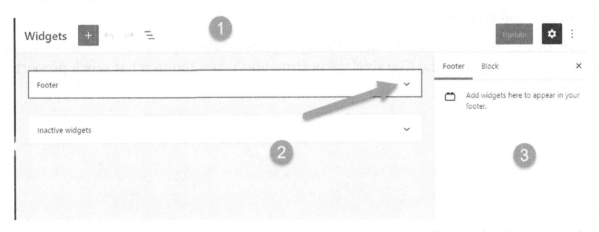

You will probably need to click the small arrow in the top right to collapse the **Footer** widget area.

The screen is split into three sections.

1. The top panel is where you can select widgets to add to an area.

2. Underneath, you can see the areas that can accept widgets. The Twenty Twenty-One has

only one widget area, and that is the footer. The Inactive widgets section will show any widgets you've created but not used. If you want to remove a widget from an area but think you might want to use it again later, those widgets can be dragged to this area for safe keeping.

3. On the right, you have access to the widget properties.

If I expand the **Footer** area, I can see any widgets added to the footer:

Note the scrollbar on the right because there are several widgets in this area. They correspond to the widgets we saw earlier in the footer area.

Widgets are standard Gutenberg Blocks, which, as you'll see later, are also the building blocks of the content you will create.

Click on any of the blocks that make up the widgets, and you'll see the familiar block menu appear above it. If you click the **Cog** settings button, you'll see the familiar block properties for the block you selected.

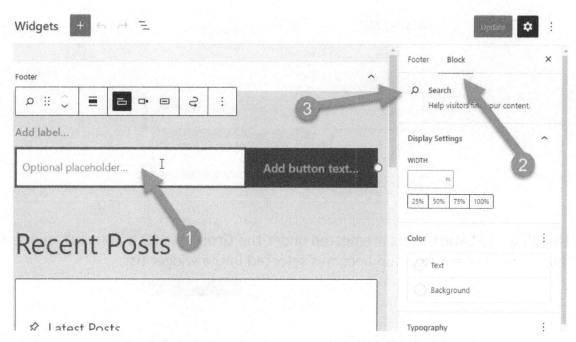

That first widget is the search box you saw in the previous screenshot. You'll notice that these properties are on the **Block** tab of the panel.

You can see at the top of the **Block** property panel that this block is called a **Search** block.

If I click on the **Recent Posts** title in the list of widgets in the footer area, I see:

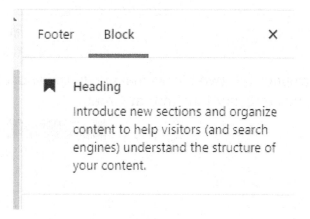

So, the Recent Posts title is added as a **Heading** block.

Click on all the elements you see in the Widgets list and watch the properties panel. You'll see that the widgets are created using different types of blocks.

The **Recent Posts** widget is made up of a **Heading** and a **Latest Posts** Block. To make handling these easier, those two blocks are grouped together inside a **Group** block. You can see this if you click the **List View** button in the toolbar consisting of three horizontal lines:

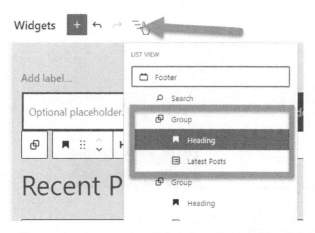

See how **Heading** and **Latest Posts** are nested under the **Group** block? If you click on the **Group** block in that menu, the entire group becomes selected in the widget list:

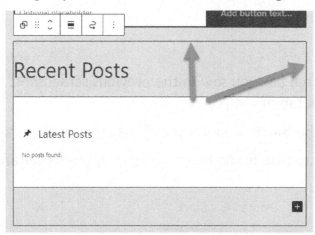

Do you see the box that surrounds the two blocks making up the widget? An **Options** menu appears, and this menu applies to everything in that Group:

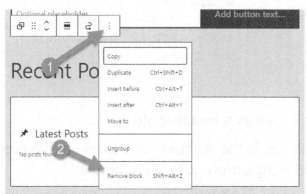

We'll look at the menu in more detail later, but for now, click the **Remove Block.** This will delete the entire group, including the **Heading** and the **Latest Posts** block.

You can also select individual blocks that are part of a group. You can do this from the **List View** menu or by clicking on the block in the main editor window. Both methods will offer the same options menu. This allows you to delete specific blocks inside groups.

Something to try

Click on the **Archives** heading and delete it using the **Options** menu. Repeat for the **Archives** block. What you'll be left with is a **Group** block with nothing inside it:

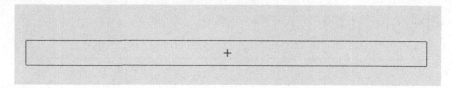

That + inside the group is an invitation to add a block to the group.

You can see this empty Group in the **List View**:

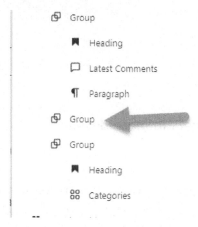

Just like any block, you can select it (directly by clicking it or via the **List** View) and then delete it using the **Options** menu.

Using a combination of **List View** and direct clicking on blocks/groups in the list, delete them all using the **Options** menu. When you are finished, it'll look something like this:

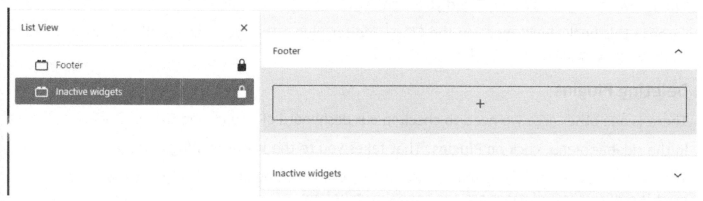

You won't be able to get rid of that last "Group" as it doesn't appear in the **List View**.

Click the **Update** button top right to save your new footer area, then go and visit your site:

29

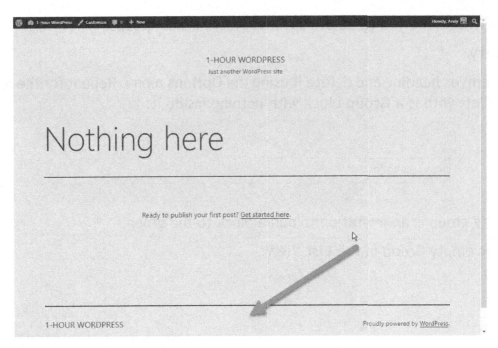

All the widgets are gone!

We'll come back later to look at Widgets in more detail.

A Note About Sidebars

The Gutenberg editor built into WordPress is designed to work with themes that use the full width of the web page to display the content you create in posts and pages. What this means is most themes created for Gutenberg, like the Twenty Twenty-One theme, don't give you the option of a sidebar.

Many older themes do have the option of a sidebar, and this is one area that was traditionally used for widgets. You can use Gutenberg as the editor for older themes, but don't be surprised if you find a few small issues as you build your content.

Later in this book, I will mention the Classic editor plugin that you can install and use instead of Gutenberg, as it does work well with sidebars.

Deleting Plugins

There is one other area we need to check in our dashboard clearout, and that is plugins.

In the sidebar menu, click on **Plugins**. That takes you to the **Installed Plugins** page.

You may or may not have any plugins pre-installed. Two common plugins that are pre-installed on most WordPress installations are the ones shown below:

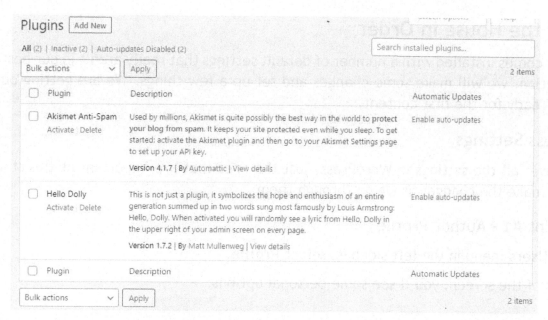

Akismet is a plugin to help you reduce spam. It is a great plugin, but it is only free if your site is not commercial in any way. If you make money from your site, you cannot use it without buying a license. Because of that, I don't cover it in this book.

The other one, Hello Dolly, simply puts quotes from the musical in the toolbar at the top of your dashboard.

You may have other plugins in your installation. Some web hosts will install plugins that are designed to improve speed and reliability on that hosting. If you do have any plugins that include the name of your web host, don't delete them. Everything else can likely be deleted (but ask your host if you are concerned about whether a plugin is essential).

Deleting a plugin properly is a two-step process:

1. If you see a **Deactivate** link under the plugin name, it means the plugin is currently running inside your dashboard.

   You need to click that deactivate link to turn it off.

2. The **Delete** link will now be visible under the plugin. Click it to delete the plugin. You will be asked to confirm the deletion. Once you confirm, the plugin is removed.

Congratulations, you have cleaned out WordPress and have an empty site waiting for you to move in.

Getting the House in Order

WordPress comes installed with a number of default settings that really aren't in our best interests. In this section, we will make some changes and set up a few things. We are getting our house in order and ready for the first content.

WordPress Settings

I won't cover all the settings in WordPress, just the ones that are important at this stage. Follow along and make the changes as we go through them.

Checkpoint #1 - Author Profile

From the **Users** menu in the left sidebar, select **Profile**.

At the top of the screen, you'll see some personal options:

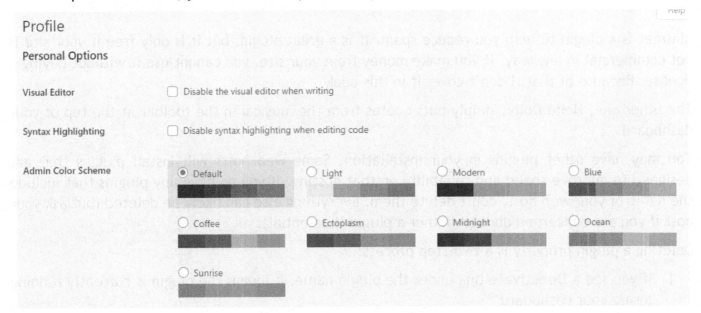

Leave the checkboxes set to their default values.

The admin color scheme is a personal taste thing, so play around with the colors if you wish.

The "Show Toolbar when viewing site" places that admin bar across the top of your browser window when you are viewing your site while logged into your Dashboard. This admin bar gives you quick access to several dashboard features.

Underneath, you need to enter a few personal details.

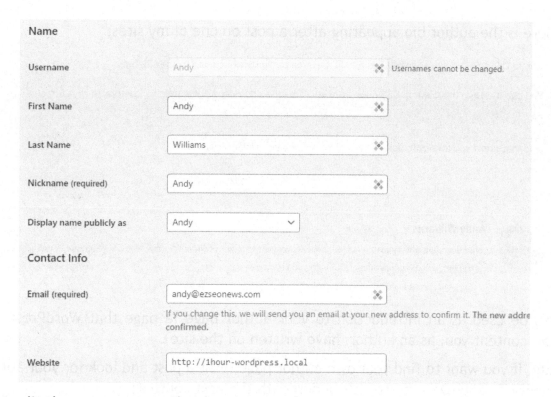

You cannot edit the username, so that box is greyed out.

Enter your first and last name.

In the Nickname, enter whatever you like. It will be prefilled with your username, but you can change it.

In the **Display name publicly as**, select the way you want your name to appear on the website. The options available will include combinations of your first and last name, nickname, username, etc.

Make sure you have a valid email address in the **Contact Info** section.

Finally, on this screen, add a little information about yourself in the **Biographical Info** box.

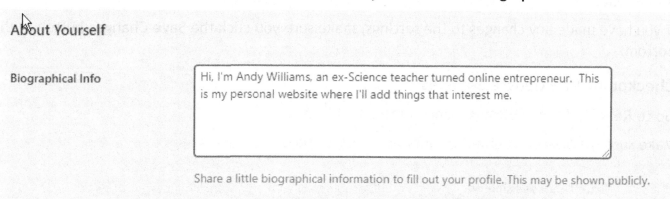

This information may be used on your website, e.g., as an author bio after posts (depending on the theme). Here is the author bio appearing after a post on one of my sites:

Create CSS to extend the content width to fill the area previously occupied by the sidebar.

You can then add this custom CSS code from your Dashboard under Appearance => Customize => Additional CSS.

And that's how you take complete control of your sidebars in WordPress.

Andy Williams

I am a Science teacher by training, but have been working online for nearly two decades, specializing in WordPress, search engine optimization and affiliate marketing. I have published a number of kindle and paperback books on Amazon and run a number of online courses. You can follow me on Facebook or Twitter.

It may also be used as an introduction to your author page (a page that WordPress creates to highlight all content you, as an author, have written on the site).

Incidentally, if you want to find your own author page, visit a post and look for your author name. On the Twenty Twenty-One theme, it's underneath the post content:

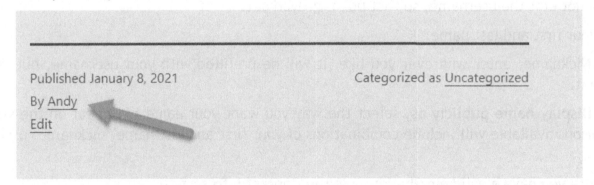

Not all themes will show this, but if it does show your "display name," click it to be taken to your author page.

If you have made any changes to the settings, make sure you click the **Save Changes** button at the bottom.

Checkpoint #2 – Update Services

Go to **Reading** in the **Settings** menu in the left sidebar.

Make sure the **Search Engine Visibility** box is unchecked:

Search engine visibility ☐ Discourage search engines from indexing this site

It is up to search engines to honor this request.

This will make sure the search engines are able to visit and index your site. If you check this box, then the search engines will ignore your site, and you won't be able to add the update services (which we are about to do).

Go to **Writing** in the **Settings** menu in the left sidebar.

You will see a large box labeled **Update Services** (also referred to as a ping list). At the moment, there is just one entry.

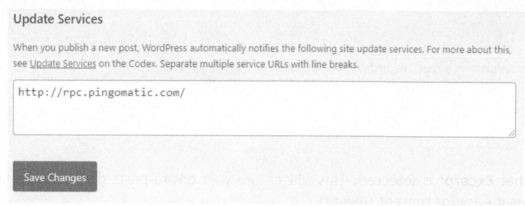

If you see this:

Update Services

WordPress is not notifying any Update Services because of your site's visibility settings.

..then you have checked the **"Search Engine Visibility"** box in the Reading settings. We covered that a moment ago.

Basically, every time you post new content (or edit old content) on your site, a message is sent to all "services" in this list (currently just Pingomatic) to let them know there is new content. They will then come over to your site to see what new content you have published.

This list helps your content get noticed and included more quickly in the search engines. WordPress installs just one service, but Pingomatic actually notifies a lot of other sites, including Google, so that one entry is fine and all I personally use.

You can find ready-made ping lists created by other website owners if you want. Just search Google for "WordPress Ping List," find a list, and paste it into the box.

Don't forget to save if you make changes before moving to the next settings page.

Checkpoint #3 - Reading Settings

Go to **Reading** in the **Settings** menu in the left sidebar:

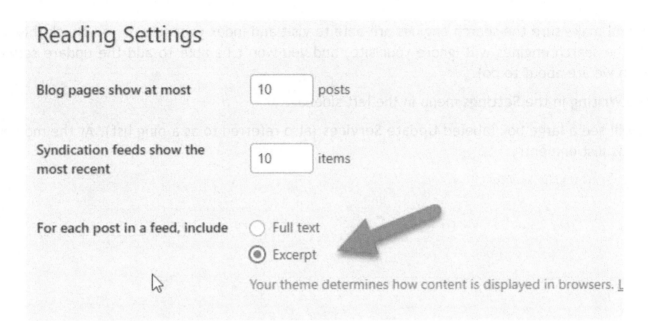

Make sure that **Excerpt** is selected. This will ensure your entire posts don't end up in RSS feeds (which makes it easy for content thieves).

Checkpoint #4 – Discussion Settings

Go to **Discussion** in the **Settings** menu in the left sidebar.

Most of these options can be left as they are. The ones to change are listed below:

Change 1:

Uncheck the option above to help prevent spammy "comments" on your site.

Change 2:

Check the option to approve all comments manually. Also, uncheck the second option (to protect against a security hack that has been used in the past).

Change 3:

The **Disallowed Comment Keys** will help sort out a lot of spam comments before you even see them. You simply enter all the words you want to be considered spam, and if those words appear in a comment, the comment is marked as spam and sent to the spam folder.

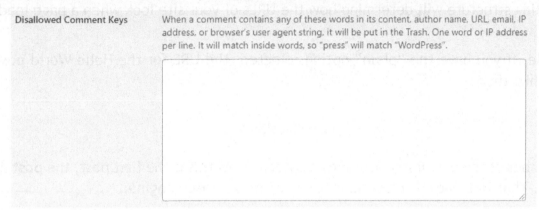

You don't have to think of the words yourself, as others have created lists for us. Do a Google search for **WordPress comment blacklist**. Find a list you can copy and paste into your own comment blacklist.

Change 4:

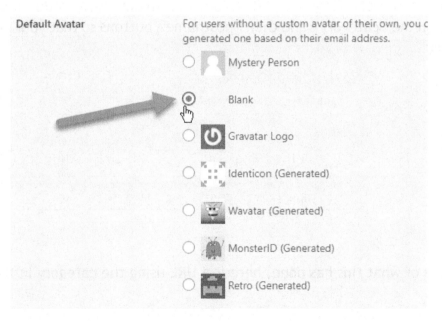

Under the **Default Avatar** section, select **Blank**.

Reason: If someone leaving a comment does not have a Gravatar set up (we will cover this in a moment), then we don't want an image displayed with their comment.

You can set it up to use any of those other images as the default image, but by using an image, you are slowing down the load times of your web pages.

Checkpoint #5 - Permalinks

Under the **Settings** menu, go to **Permalinks**.

This is an important one.

The permalink structure will determine how the URLs of your site look when a page loads in a web browser.

For example, if you have the "plain" option selected, the URL for the Hello World post will look something like this:

> 1-hour-wordpress.local/?p=1

P is the number of the post in the WordPress database. As this is the first post, the **post ID** of "hello world" is 1. That URL doesn't offer much to a visitor or search engine.

From a search engine point of view, it is far better to be more descriptive with your URLs. If you are going to be using a few different categories on your site, I'd recommend you include the category in the permalink. If you are only using one category, leave it out and move on, as the default setting is %postname%, which is fine for you.

If you are using a number of categories, select **Custom Structure**, and deselect the %Postname% button. Now click on the %category% and then %postname% buttons so that your permalink structure now looks like this:

Save your changes.

To give you an idea of what this has done, here is a URL using the category in the URL :

> https://andyjwilliams.co.uk/animals/dogs/jessie/

The postname, in this case, is called "Jessie." The main category is "animals," and the sub-category is "dogs."

Checkpoint #6 - Gravatars

We mentioned Gravatars when going through the **Discussion Settings**. Gravatars are images that we can associate with our email addresses. If you look at the top right of your Dashboard, you will see your name and a placeholder image where your photo could be. Here is mine:

My photo appears there because I am using a Gravatar associated with my admin email address. If I use that email to post a comment on any other blog, my photo appears with my comment. Here is an example:

ANDY WILLIAMS
27/3/2019 AT 11:04

This was my understanding. Thanks for the info Eva.

Edit

In the screenshot, I am replying to a comment. My Gravatar shows because I used an admin email address that I had linked to that image.

Gravatars are a great way to brand yourself, and I highly recommend you use a Gravatar for your own Admin email address. Visitors to your site love to know who they are dealing with, so get over your shyness and put your face on your site.

To sign up for a Gravatar, head on over to https://en.gravatar.com/

Look for the link to **Create your own Gravatar**, and follow the instructions. Now, whenever you post a comment on any website that is related to your own, use the email address that has your Gravatar attached, and your face will show up next to your comments on these other sites (unless they have Gravatars disabled, but very few do).

Checkpoint #8 – Adding a Sitemap

A sitemap is essentially a list of pages on your site, and it is used mainly by search engines to find all your content. It is, therefore, a good idea to have one. The best way to add a sitemap is to use a plugin.

Click on **Add New** in the **Plugins** sidebar menu.

Search for **Yoast SEO** and find this plugin by Team Yoast:

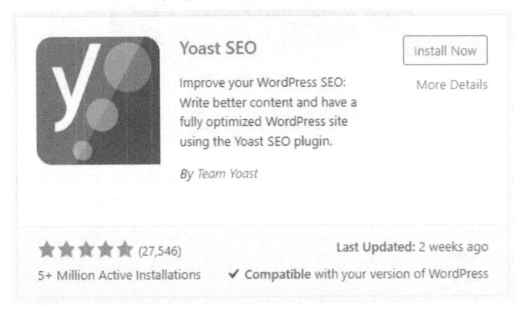

Click the **Install Now**.

Once installed, click the **Activate** button that replaced the "install now" button.

You will now have a new sidebar menu:

As the menu title suggests, this plugin is more than a sitemap plugin. It's a very flexible and useful SEO plugin. It is beyond the scope of this book to teach you how to set this up, but I will show you how to activate the sitemap.

Click on the **Settings** menu and scroll down the screen until you find the APIs section:

APIs

REST API endpoint

This Yoast SEO REST API endpoint gives you all the metadata you need for a specific URL. This will make it very easy for headless WordPress sites to use Yoast SEO for all their SEO meta output.

Learn more →

Enable feature ◉

XML sitemaps

Enable the Yoast SEO XML sitemaps. A sitemap is a file that lists a website's essential pages to make sure search engines can find and crawl them.

[View the XML sitemap ⧉]

Learn more →

Enable feature ◉

You'll see a panel dedicated to the sitemap. Make sure it is enabled.

To see your sitemap, click the **View the XML Sitemap** button:

XML Sitemap

Generated by Yoast SEO, this is an XML Sitemap, meant for consumption by search engines.

You can find more information about XML sitemaps on sitemaps.org.

This XML Sitemap Index file contains 3 sitemaps.

Sitemap	Last Modified
http://1-hour-wordpress.local/post-sitemap.xml	2023-02-20 11:43 +00:00
http://1-hour-wordpress.local/category-sitemap.xml	2023-02-20 11:43 +00:00
http://1-hour-wordpress.local/author-sitemap.xml	2023-02-20 11:50 +00:00

If you get a 404 error, meaning the page does not exist, make sure:

1. You have posts on your site that are published.

2. You have saved the permalink structure (even if you did not change it).

With a working sitemap, whenever you add a new post to your site, it will automatically be added to this sitemap. Google and any other sites in your "ping list" will automatically be notified of the new content. You should find that once your site becomes established, new content will be indexed and found in Google within minutes of you clicking the "publish" button.

As we are getting close to adding content to the site, let's start to think about that content and create a preliminary plan.

Planning the site

We've got a skeleton site with no content. The first thing I suggest you do is to plan out what you want to include on your site. What content do you want to publish there?

Before we start, there is something I want you to think about as you plan out your site. We have just finished clearing out some pre-installed content. Remember, there were WordPress **posts** and WordPress **pages**. Both posts and pages can be used to create a web page. What is the difference? When do we use a post, and when do we use a page? We will answer these questions in time, but for now, I don't want you to worry too much about the differences. I just want you to plan out your site with a quick sketch showing the types of content you intend to create.

You don't have to decide on everything just yet, but having a good plan before you start will make things a lot easier.

WordPress is so flexible that you can use it to create just about any type of website.

Let's consider a simple model for a site I might create to teach WordPress:

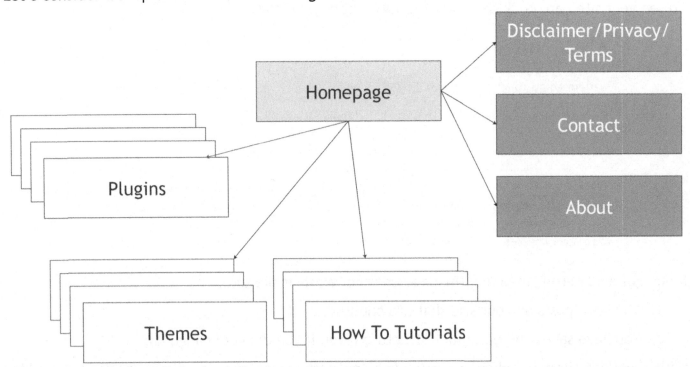

The homepage will introduce the site to the visitors and tell them what the site is about. The homepage will also help them find what they are looking for. The site might have three main sections containing groups of related web pages.

There will be a group of web pages, each discussing a different plugin that you can use with WordPress.

There will also be a group of web pages, each discussing a different WordPress theme.

Then the final group of web pages will be tutorials showing how to do the stuff a WordPress site owner needs to do.

In addition to this website "content," there are a few other things you need:

1. About Us page.

2. Contact Us form.

3. Privacy Policy.

4. Terms of Use.

I tend to call the pages like disclaimer, terms, and contact, the "legal pages." These "legal" pages are typically very similar for all sites you build, irrespective of the topic.

From the above, we can see that there are two distinct types of content.

There are those articles that can typically and conveniently be grouped into "categories" because they are all related to a particular topic. When a group of articles can be grouped into a category, you create those articles using WordPress **posts**.

The other type of content is the stuff that is not directly related to the topic of the site but is required to make the site complete and more professional (as well as provide ourselves with a little legal protection). This type of web page is not strongly related to any other piece of content. These web pages are not something you would think of grouping into a category. When a piece of content is more stand-alone and cannot be grouped into a tightly related category, we use a WordPress **page** for the content.

Are you starting to see the difference between WordPress posts and WordPress pages?

Let's look at these differences in more detail.

Pages v Posts

WordPress gives you two options for adding new content to your site. These are confusingly called "Pages" and "Posts."

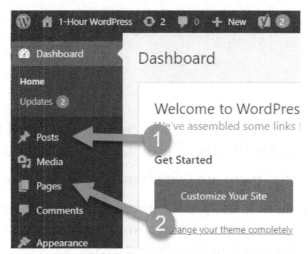

Both use the exact same content editor, making it easy to add content. However, you need to decide which one and when to use each.

I've already hinted at when to use pages and when to use posts earlier in this book, but I'd like to revisit this topic and explain the differences between pages and posts.

From now on, whenever I talk about posts, I am referring to WordPress POSTS, and whenever I talk about pages, I am referring to WordPress PAGES.

WordPress was originally designed with bloggers in mind, and WordPress "posts" were the tool given to the blogger so they could add updates to the blog. These WordPress posts were designed to be date-dependent so that posts could be listed in chronological order. Think of it much like a diary. Things happen, and you enter them in the order they happen. If you then ordered the posts in date order, with the oldest posts at the top, you'd have a chronological list of posts over time. This was how posts were originally designed to be used.

So, what about WordPress "pages"?

Well, pages are not date-dependent. They are standalone pages, and each page is usually unrelated to any other piece of content on the site. Remember I said that "legal" pages should be pages? Can you see why?

Post Categories

A major difference between posts and pages is that posts can be grouped and categorized (reinforcing the idea that posts can be related to other posts), whereas pages cannot (this isn't strictly true, but it helps if you think it is).

Remember the website structure I mapped out earlier for a site about WordPress?

There were a number of related articles about various WordPress plugins. There were also a bunch of related articles reviewing WordPress themes. The beauty of grouping and categorizing content on your site is that WordPress makes it easy to manipulate these groups of posts and treat them as a related whole.

For example, if a visitor lands on my review of the Astra WordPress theme, doesn't it make sense to show that visitor a list of other theme reviews to give them more information before they choose one to buy?

WordPress makes this easy with posts, but there is no easy, built-in way of doing this with WordPress pages. Pages were designed to be separate, standalone pieces of content unrelated to anything else on the site.

All posts are given a category, whereas pages are not. Earlier in this book, I showed you the URL of a post after we made the change to the permalink structure.

🔒   https://andyjwilliams.co.uk/animals/dogs/jessie/

This post is in the dogs sub-category of the main animal category.

Here is another URL on the same site:

https://andyjwilliams.co.uk/animals/birds/kingfisher/

This URL is for a post about Kingfishers. It's placed in a sub-category of Animals called "Birds."

And this one:

https://andyjwilliams.co.uk/animals/birds/robin/

This is a post about robins. It's in the birds sub-category of the Animals category.

Do you see how categories are helping to organize my content?

If someone goes to my animals category, they'll see all posts about animals. If they only want to see the bird posts, they can go to the animals/birds category instead.

Let's think about how we might structure the posts on my fictional site teaching WordPress:

Some of the URLs might include:

```
https://1hour-wordpress.local/plugins/yarpp
https://1hour-wordpress.local/plugins/elementor
https://1hour-wordpress.local/plugins/akismet
https://1hour-wordpress.local/plugins/yoast-seo
https://1hour-wordpress.local/themes/astra
https://1hour-wordpress.local/themes/twenty-twenty-one
https://1hour-wordpress.local/themes/avada
https://1hour-wordpress.local/tutorials/how-to-install-wordpress
https://1hour-wordpress.local/tutorials/how-to-stop-spammers
```

.. and so on. You can instantly see that groups of posts are related because of the category in the

URL.

This is a major SEO (Search Engine Optimization) benefit of posts as well. The search engines see these posts in the same category, and this helps them categorize and rank your content. The search engines know that these groups of posts are related, and carefully selected categories will help them categorize and rank your pages accordingly.

WordPress actually helps out even more.

For every category you create (I have three in the example above), WordPress creates a "category page" that lists all posts in that category. Therefore, WordPress will create a category page for plugins, one for themes, and another for tutorials.

The category page URLs will look like this:

```
https://1hour-wordpress.local/category/plugins
https://1hour-wordpress.local/category/themes
https://1hour-wordpress.local/category/tutorials
```

Looking at the URL list above, the plugins category page would currently list four posts, the themes category page would list 3, and the tutorials category page would list 2.

The search engines know that WordPress category pages list related posts, so it automatically knows that all posts listed on a category page are related by theme.

A post can be given more than one category. However, I don't recommend it. Categories are the top level of organization of posts, and I want you to stick to only using ONE category per post.

Why?

Well, what would a search engine "think" if a post was in two categories? It would probably wonder what the post was about, category 1 or category 2.

However, what if I had a category called "reviews"?

My "theme" posts could then go into both the themes category and the reviews category.

Similarly, my plugin reviews could go into the plugin category AND the review category.

If you have this dilemma, then you probably need to re-assess your category structure. However, WordPress does give us another tool that can help solve this problem.

Tags!

Post Tags

So, categories are the main way we categorize and group posts. WordPress also gives us a secondary method for categorizing content called **Tags**. These are just words or phrases we can assign to a post, like keywords related to the post. So, we could "tag" all review posts as "reviews" while keeping them in tightly focused categories.

Just as WordPress creates a "category page" for all categories you define, it also creates a tag page for each tag you use. For example, if you tagged 5 of your posts with the tag "review," then WordPress would create a review tag page that lists those five posts. The URL would look like this:

```
http://1hour-wordpress.local/tag/review/
```

On the review tag page of my WordPress site, we would see every post on the site that had been tagged with "review." That means posts across multiple categories. Can you see the power of this? It's an extra level of organization!

A post can have multiple tags assigned to it, but only create tags if they are going to be used on multiple posts. Never use a tag that will only appear in one post.

The rule is that each post should only be in ONE category but can have multiple tags.

Let me give you an example of when you might use a tag.

Suppose you have a site about vacuum cleaners. You have decided on categories like Dyson, Hoover, Eureka, Kirby, Dirt Devil, and so on. In other words, you are using the manufacturer names as categories. All Dyson vacuum reviews go in the Dyson category, and all Kirby reviews go in the Kirby category.

This makes sense because, as the webmaster, you decided that most visitors know the brand of vacuum they want, so grouping by the brand helps them more easily find the model that suits them best. To find a Dyson, they can simply go to your Dyson category page, where all Dyson reviews are listed.

However, sometimes visitors do not know the brand of vacuum they want. All they know is that they want a hand-held vacuum, or a canister vacuum, or maybe a vacuum designed to deal with pet hair.

This is where I would use tags.

I'd have the following tags:

- upright
- canister
- pets
- hand-held
- HEPA filter
- etc.

Therefore, my Dyson DC31 Animal review would be put in the Dyson category, but I could tag it with pets and hand-held.

The beauty of tags is that we can manipulate them in the same way we do categories. If someone on your site is interested in "hand-held vacuums" but not sure which manufacturer, you can show them a list of all vacuums "tagged" with "hand-held."

As mentioned earlier, WordPress creates a "tag page" for each tag you use. Each tag page lists all posts that have used that tag. So WordPress would create a page that lists all "hand-held" vacuum reviews.

Sound familiar? Yes, it's very much like the category pages we mentioned earlier.

So, posts can have categories and tags assigned to them.

I do have a few rules on using categories and tags efficiently. These rules will keep you out of trouble. Here they are:

1. Only one category per post.

2. You can have multiple tags, but try to limit each post to 5 or fewer tags. The more tags you use in a post, the more spammy your site begins to look to Google.

3. Never use a tag if only one post will be tagged with it. I personally only create a tag if it will be used on a minimum of three posts. Tags, like categories, are there to help organize and group your posts. If there is only one post using a tag, it's not a group. Remember that WordPress creates a "tag page" for each tag you use. If you only have one post using a tag, then that tag page will basically just contain one post. That would be considered duplicate content by Google since you already have that one post on its own "post page," as well as on a category page.

4. Never create a tag with the same name as a category.

Tags are ultimately there to help you make your site better for your visitors. Don't abuse them.

Post Excerpts

Another great feature of posts is that they can have **Excerpts**. Pages cannot.

These are short descriptions of the article that can be used by themes and plugins to create a Meta description tag or a description of the article in a list of related articles. For example, below is a related posts section (created using a plugin) on one of my websites. It shows excerpts being used for the post descriptions:

Related Posts

You can add an excerpt for a post on the edit post screen. Look for the field in the right-hand sidebar:

If you don't write an excerpt, plugins and themes may grab a bit of text from your post to use as the description. This won't be a complete sentence and can look really unprofessional.

You can see how using excerpts makes your site look more professional and better for your visitors. It also allows you to write some unique text that will act as a description to entice visitors.

Posts and RSS Feeds

Another important difference between posts and pages is that posts appear in RSS feeds, but pages do not.

WordPress sites automatically create RSS feeds. These are special files that contain a list of the most recent posts on your site.

WordPress creates a single RSS feed for your entire site, but it also creates separate feeds for each category, each tag, all posts by a particular author, etc.

To see an RSS feed of your site, type in your domain name followed by **/feed** like this:

You can try this on any WordPress website, not just those you own.

RSS feeds are important tools to notify people, and other websites, that you have published new content. Personally, I monitor the RSS feeds (using a free service over at Feedly.com) of my favorite websites, and when they post new content, the feed is updated (automatically by WordPress), and I get notified of that new content.

When to Use Posts and When to Use Pages

OK, this is the million-dollar question that I get asked a lot!

This will depend on the type of website you want to build, and we will mention this again later in the book when we discuss website structure again.

A Blog?

A lot of people want to create a Blog with WordPress. A blog is typically a regularly updated website written in an informal or conversational style. Here is a typical blog structure:

A Typical Blog

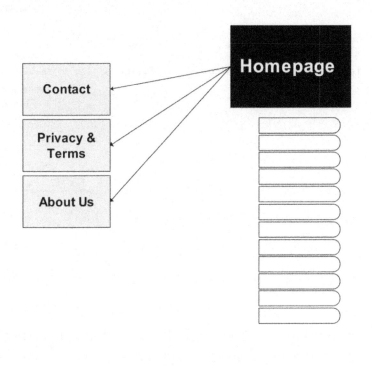

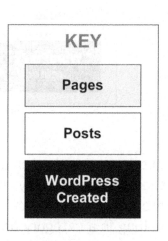

We use WordPress pages for the legal pages and the About us. The blog posts themselves are all created using WordPress posts, and these are organized by WordPress on the homepage of the site, which is created and maintained by WordPress. This is the default structure of a site when you start working with WordPress.

A Business Site?

For a lot of business websites, using pages for most of the content makes sense, like this:

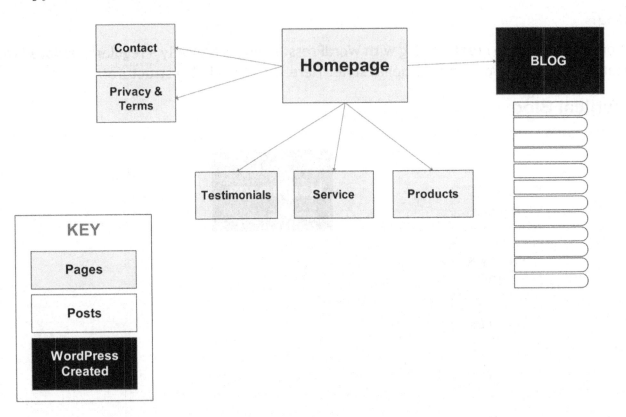

In this model, the company site uses WordPress "pages" for all of the main important content that they want to convey to visitors. So homepage, contact, legal pages, testimonials, services, and products. These pieces of content are all isolated and unrelated to the other pages. They don't belong in a category or group in any way. And that is where a page comes in useful.

The company site also has a blog built with posts. WordPress creates and maintains that blog page for us, listing the most recent posts.

From the point of view of this company, what features of posts make them ideal for the blog?

Probably the fact they are chronological, so recent posts appear at the top of the blog. Definitely the fact that the blog posts appear in the RSS feed, so anyone monitoring the feeds will be notified of the new blog post.

A Typical Niche Site?

The main type of website I personally build uses a different model. It is a model that particularly suits niche sites, eCommerce, etc. It's a model that relies on the fact that a piece of content does not live on an island; it is related to other pieces of content, which can be grouped and categorized.

This model offers great SEO benefits, as well as organizing content in a logical manner to help both visitors and search engines. Here is a diagram of the model:

A Typical Niche Site

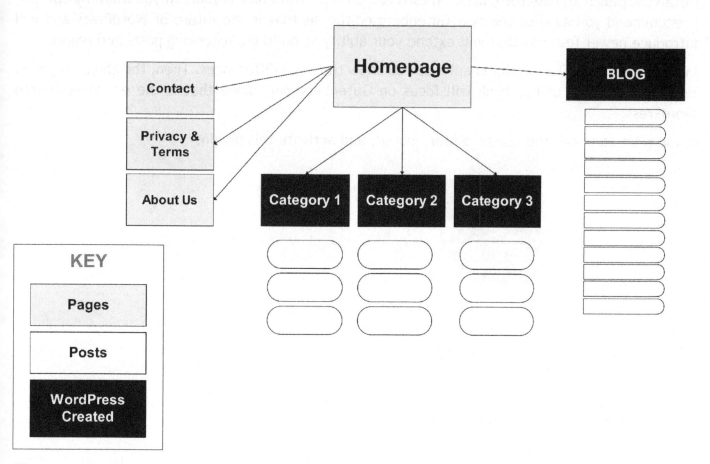

The main legal pages are created with Pages. Again, this makes sense as these pages are not something you would group or categorize in any way.

The blog is created using posts. There are also a number of categories used to group related content.

In a model like this, where we want to use categories and have a completely separate blog, the easiest way to achieve this is to create a category called "blog" and put all blog posts in that category. You know that WordPress will create a category page for the blog category, so your blog becomes the "blog" category page.

Writing Posts

In this section of the book, I want to look at publishing content on your site. Version 5.0 of WordPress changed things dramatically. The old WYSIWYG editor (now called the Classic editor) was replaced by a page builder system called Gutenberg.

The two systems are VERY different.

The good news is that with the introduction of Gutenberg, WordPress created a "Classic Editor" plugin that can be installed, so you have a choice. You can use the new Gutenberg page builder or install the plugin and use the classic "WYSIWYG" editor. The choice is yours. If you want my opinion, I recommend you go with the new Gutenberg editor, as that is the future of WordPress and will introduce newer features that will extend your ability to build great-looking posts and pages.

I will cover both editors in this chapter so you know the main differences. Then, the choice is yours. However, the rest of the book will focus on Gutenberg only since that is the editor built into WordPress.

If you want to install the Classic editor, install, and activate this plugin:

Once installed, click on the **Settings** link:

The plugin has added its settings to the **Writing** settings page, which makes sense considering this plugin helps you write content. There are two main settings you can change:

The first one defines which editor you want to use by default. The Block editor option refers to Gutenberg. The second option is whether you want users to be able to switch back and forth between the Classic Editor and Gutenberg.

Choosing the Classic Editor or Gutenberg

If you want to use Gutenberg, then don't install the Classic Editor plugin. All posts and pages will then be created in the Gutenberg editor.

If you want to use the classic editor, install and activate the plugin. All "add post" and "add page" links will then default to the Classic editor.

Let's look at how you can add content, first using the Classic editor, then using Gutenberg. If you installed the Classic Editor plugin, then follow along. If you are intent on only using Gutenberg, then ignore this section.

The "Classic" WYSIWYG Editor

Click **Add New** in the **Posts** menu.

The Classic editor looks like this:

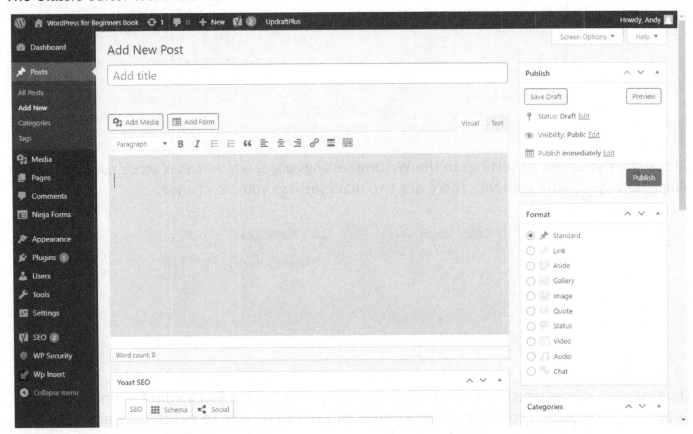

There is a box for the title and a large editor box for writing the content:

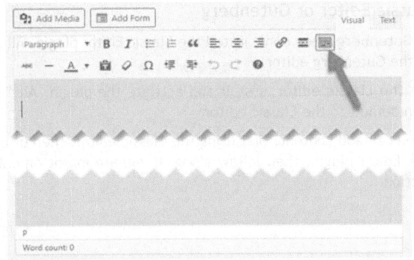

If you only see one line of buttons on your toolbar, click the **Toggle Toolbar** button on the far right. That will expand the toolbar.

You'll see on the top right there are two tabs, above and to the right of the toolbar – **Visual** & **Text**.

The Visual tab is where you can write your content using WYSIWYG features. On this tab, you'll see text and media formatted as they will appear on the website once published. This is the tab you will want to use for most of the work you do when adding new or editing existing content on your site.

The other tab – Text - shows the raw code that is responsible for the layout and content of the page. Unless you specifically need to insert some code or script into your content, stick with the Visual tab.

The two rows of buttons allow you to format your content visually. If you have used any type of Word Processor before, then this should be intuitive.

I won't go through the functions of all these buttons. If you need help understanding what a button does, move your mouse over it to get a popup help tooltip.

Adding content to your site is as easy as typing it into the large box under the toolbar. Just use it like you would any word processor.

Write your content. Select some text and click a formatting button to apply the format. Make it bold, change its color, make it a header, or any of the other features offered in the toolbar.

To create a headline, enter the headline and press the return button on your keyboard to make sure it is on its own line. Now click somewhere in the headline and select the headline from the drop-down box in the toolbar.

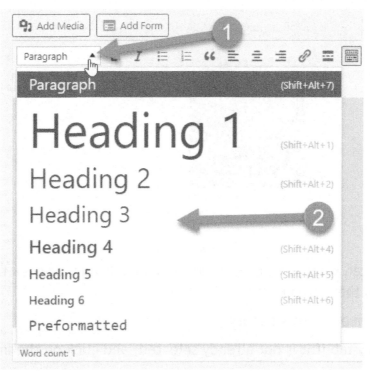

NOTE: WordPress themes typically show the title of your post as an H1 header at the top of the page. This is the biggest header available and is equivalent to **Heading 1** in the drop-down selector. You should not use more than one H1 header on a web page, so avoid using **Heading 1** as you write your content. Use **Heading 2** for the main sections within your article and **Heading 3** for sub-headers inside **Heading 2** sections.

OK, it's now time to go ahead and write the post for your website.

As you write your article, you may want to insert an image or some other form of media. We looked at the Media library earlier in the book, but let's go through the process of adding an image to an article.

Adding Images

The process is straightforward.

Position your cursor in the article where you want to add the image. Don't worry too much about getting it in the right place because you can always re-position it later if you need to.

Click the **Add Media** button located above the WYSIWYG editor to the left, and you'll see the popup screen that we've seen previously:

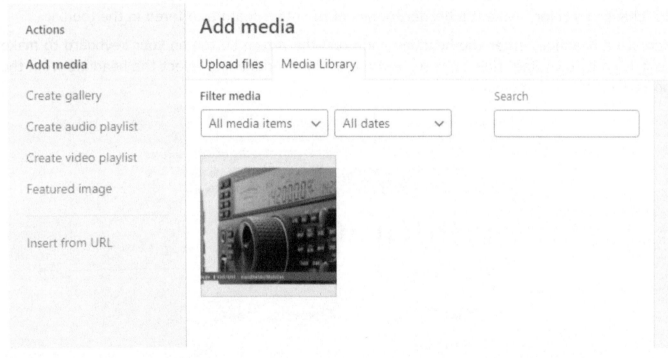

From this screen, you can select an image from the media library or click the **Upload Files** tab to upload a new image to the media library.

Let's add an image from our Media Library.

Click the **Media Library** tab if it is not already selected, and click on the image you want to use in the post.

A checkmark appears in the top right corner of the image, and the "attachment" details are displayed on the right side. These image details can be edited if you want to.

At the bottom of the right sidebar is an **Insert into post** button. Before you click that, we should consider a few of the sidebar options.

One important option is the **Alt Text**. This text is read to the visually impaired visitors on your site and helps them understand what images are being shown. Therefore, add a short descriptive ALT text. For my example, **Kenwood Radio** is sufficient.

At the bottom of the right-hand column (you may need to scroll down) are some **Attachment Display Settings**. Currently, my image is set to "none" for alignment.

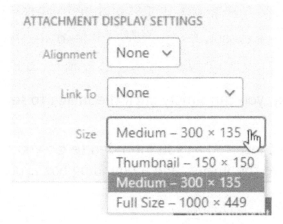

I want to align the image to the left so I can select that from the drop-down box. When an image is aligned left (or right) in WordPress, the post text wraps around it. If you select **None** or **Center** for alignment, the text won't wrap.

The next option you have is to link your image to something. The default setting is **None**, meaning we insert an image that is not clickable by the visitor because it is not linked to anything. Most of the time, I'll use none. However, if you want the image to open when clicked (e.g., in a lightbox), then select **Media file**.

You can also link an image to an **Attachment page** (which we saw earlier) or a **Custom URL**.

The **Custom URL** option is useful. This allows you to navigate to a URL when a user clicks an image. For example, if your image is a "Buy Now" button, you'd want the image linked to the purchase page.

The last of the display settings is **Size**. You'll be able to choose from a range of available options.

The dimensions are included with each file size, so choose the one that is closest to the size you want the image to appear on your page.

Once you have made your selection, click the **Insert into post** button.

Here is that image inserted into my post at the position of my cursor:

If you have the position wrong, you can simply click the image to select it and drag the image to a different location.

If you find that the image isn't inserted as you intended (e.g., you forgot to align it), click on the image. A toolbar appears above the image, and a bounding box around it:

The bounding box includes a small square in each corner. You can use this to resize the image. Drag one of the corners to make the image bigger or smaller.

The first four buttons in the toolbar allow you to re-align the image.

The last button in the toolbar will delete the image.

The toolbar edit button looks like a pencil. You can use this to open the **Image Details** screen to make several changes:

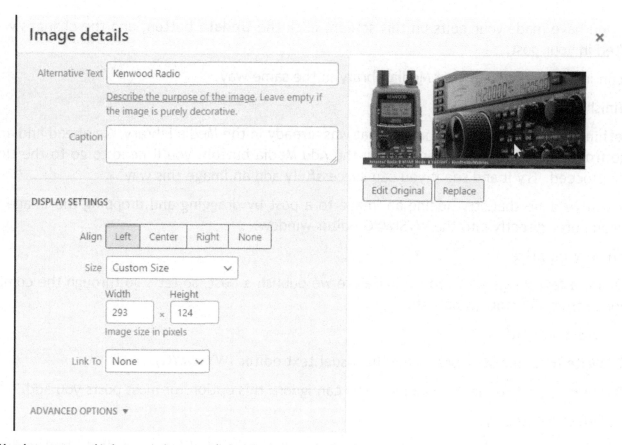

You'll also see a link to **Advanced Options** at the bottom. Click that to expand the advanced options:

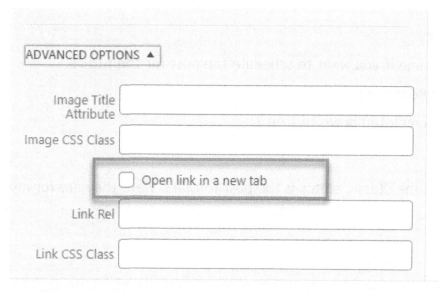

One of the most useful advanced options is the **Open link in a new tab** option. When someone clicks the image, whatever it is linked to opens in a new browser tab.

Once you have made your edits on this screen, click the **Update** button, and the changes will be updated in your post.

You can insert videos from your Media library in the same way.

OK, finish your first post.

Something to try: We added an image that was already in the Media Library. Go ahead and add an image from your hard disk. After clicking the Add Media button, you'll need to go to the Upload tab to proceed. Try it and see if you can successfully add an image this way.

Once you've done that, try adding an image to a post by dragging and dropping the image from your computer directly into the WYSIWYG editor window.

It's all very intuitive.

There are a few things we need to do before we publish a post, so let's go through the complete sequence from the start to publish:

1. Add a post title.

2. Write & format your post using the visual text editor (WYSIWYG).

3. Select a post format if available. You can ignore this option for most posts you add.

4. Select a category.

5. Add some tags if you want to. Tags can always be added later, so don't feel under any pressure to add them now. Of course, you can also decide you don't want to use tags on your site. That is fine too.

6. Add an excerpt.

7. Select a date/time if you want to schedule the post for the future.

8. Publish/Schedule the post.

OK, so far, we have completed down to step 2.

Post Formats

One of the sections in the Classic editor is the post formats. Here they are for my Twenty Twenty-One theme:

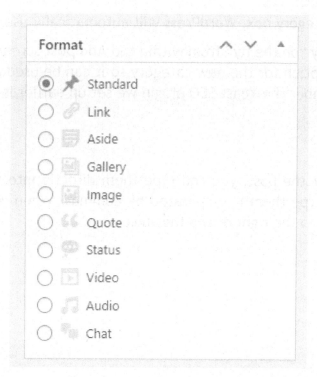

Post formats are different layouts built into the theme. When you have entered a post, play around with the post format, and see what effect each format has on the layout and style.

Most people never get around to using post formats, but it is nice to know they are there if you need them.

If you are interested in post formats, you can read more about them on the WordPress websites:

https://wordpress.org/support/article/post-formats/

Post Category

The next step in our publishing sequence is to choose a category. Choose just one category for each post.

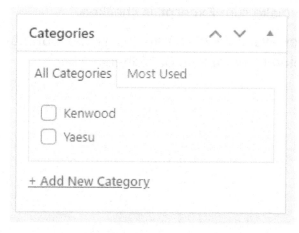

If you forget to check a category box, WordPress will automatically use your default category.

You can add a new category "on the fly" from within the **Add post** screen, but if you do, remember to go in and write a description for the new category so it can be used as the meta description of that category page (remember the Yoast SEO plugin we set up earlier is expecting a description of categories and tags).

Post Tags

If you want to use tags for the post, you can type them directly into the tags box, even if they don't already exist. Just type them in, separated by commas. When you are finished typing the tags, click the **Add** button to the right of the tags box.

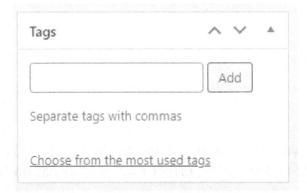

As you add and use more tags, you can click on **Choose from the most used tags,** and a box will appear with some of the tags you've used before. You can just click the tags that apply, and they'll be added to the tag list of your post.

If you add new tags when entering a post, remember to go into the Tags settings to write a short description for each one. Yes, it takes time, but it is worth that description on the tag page.

Post Excerpt

You should add a post excerpt to all posts. If you don't see an excerpt entry box on your screen, check the **Screen Options** to make sure **Excerpt** is checked.

NOTE: Screen options are not available if you are using the Gutenberg editor, but that doesn't matter, as excerpts are enabled by default in Gutenberg.

Screen elements

Some screen elements can be shown or hidden by using the checkboxes. They can be expanded and collapsed by clickling on their and arranged by dragging their headings or by clicking on the up and down arrows.

☑ Format ☑ Categories ☑ Tags ☑ Append a Ninja Form ☑ Featured image ☑ Yoast SEO ☑ Excerpt ☐ Send 1

☐ Custom Fields ☐ Discussion ☐ Slug ☐ Author

Layout

○ 1 column ● 2 columns

Additional settings

Once checked, the **Excerpt** box magically appears at the bottom of your edit post screen.

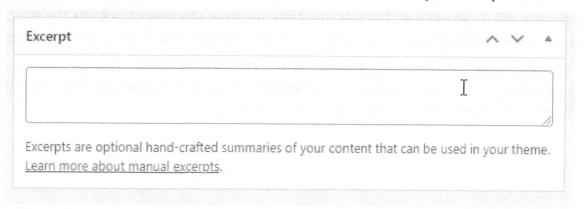

The excerpt should be a short description of the post you are writing. Its purpose is to encourage visitors to click through and read the article (e.g., From the search engine). This excerpt will be used as the Meta description tag of the post, as well as the description of the post in the "related posts" section, which is displayed at the end of each article you publish (see the YARPP plugin later).

Enter a three to five-sentence excerpt that encourages the click.

Publishing the Post

The next step in the process is deciding when you want the post to go live on your site. Let's look at the **Publish** section of the screen.

The first option you have is to save the post as a draft.

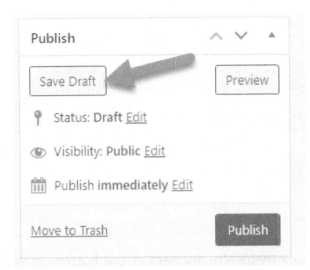

Once saved as a draft, you can go back at any time to make changes or publish the article. Draft posts are not shown on your site. To be visible on your website, you need to publish the post.

If you want it up there immediately, then click the Publish button. If, like me, you are writing several posts in a batch, it is a good idea to spread the posting of the content out a little bit. Luckily, WordPress allows us to schedule posts in the future.

The default is to publish **immediately**. However, there is an **Edit** link you can click to open a scheduling calendar:

Enter the date and time you want to publish the post, and then click the OK button.

The publish button now changes to **Schedule**.

Click the **Schedule** button to schedule the post.

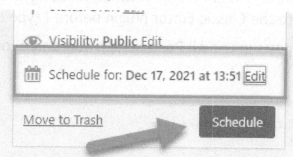

That's it. You've just published or scheduled your first WordPress post using the Classic editor.

If you now click on **All Posts** in the sidebar menu, you will see your new post listed. If you selected the option to allow users to switch editors (when we set up the Classic editor plugin), you are given the option of editing the post in the Classic Editor (which created the post) or the Block Editor (Gutenberg).

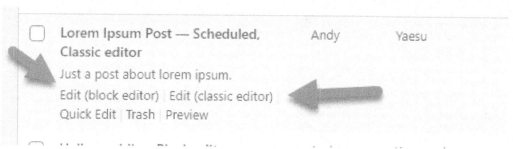

If you did not select the option to allow switching of the editor, you'd just have a single standard edit link. If you need to change that setting, go to the Writing settings to make the change, and don't forget to save those changes.

The Gutenberg Editor

Gutenberg is the default editor in WordPress, so I will be focusing on it from now on. In fact, I am going to deactivate and delete the Classic Editor plugin before I type another word.

OK, that's done. My table of posts in the **All Posts** screen now only shows the Edit/Quick Edit links:

	Title	Author	Categories
☐			
☐	**Kenwood Radio — Scheduled** Lorem ipsum dolor sit amet, consectetur adipiscing elit. In interdum risus et nunc aliquam, at fermentum nisi tincidunt. Edit | Quick Edit | Trash | Preview	Andy	Kenwood
☐	Kenwood TS- Edit | Quick Edit | Trash | View	Andy	Kenwood
☐	**Hello world!** Welcome to WordPress. This is your first post. Edit or delete it, then start writing! Edit | Quick Edit | Trash | View	Andy	Yaesu

The **Edit** link will open the post in the Gutenberg editor (because I removed the Classic plugin editor). If you want to stick with Gutenberg, I recommend you remove the Classic Editor plugin too.

If you've ever used a WordPress "page builder" like Elementor, then Gutenberg will seem a lot more familiar to you. Like other page builders, Gutenberg uses a system of blocks to help you build your content.

When you now open a post or page that was created with the Classic editor, any content you created in the Classic editor will be contained in a single **Classic Block**. You can see this if you open the **List View**:

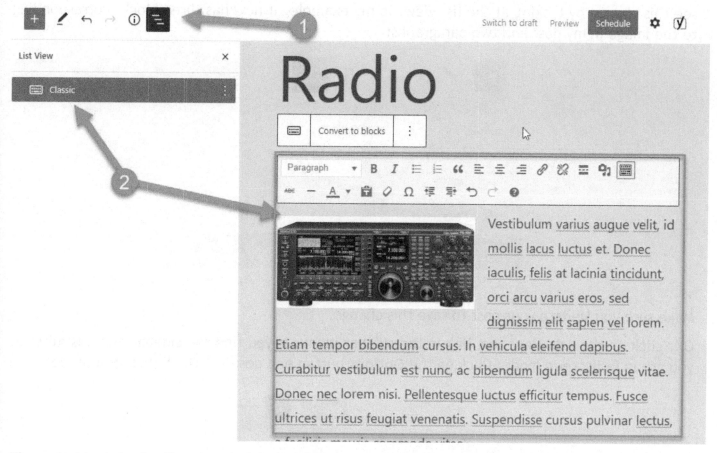

The only block in the list view is labeled "Classic." Clicking on it in the list view will select it in the editor, and you'll see the classic style menu above this block.

The good news is that we can convert these classic blocks to Gutenberg blocks. Above the classic block menu is a button labeled **Convert to blocks**.

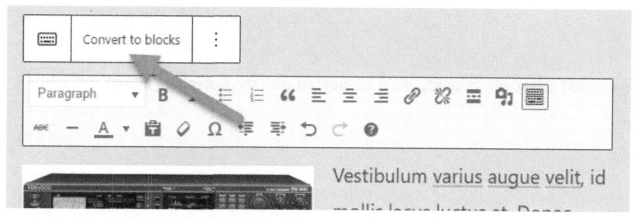

Since we are now working exclusively with Gutenberg, click that button.

You'll find that the content will now be divided up into discrete Gutenberg blocks. Each block can now be selected and manipulated in isolation from the rest of the content. You can more easily see this change by looking at the list view. In my example, it now has three blocks corresponding to the image in my post and two paragraphs:

Make sure you **Update** your post to save this change.

OK, click on the **Add New** post link in the sidebar menu. If you find the sidebar menu is missing, you are in **Fullscreen** mode. Click on the **Options** button and deselect the **Fullscreen mode**.

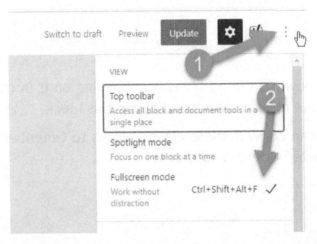

When you add a new post or page, you'll be greeted with the Gutenberg editor:

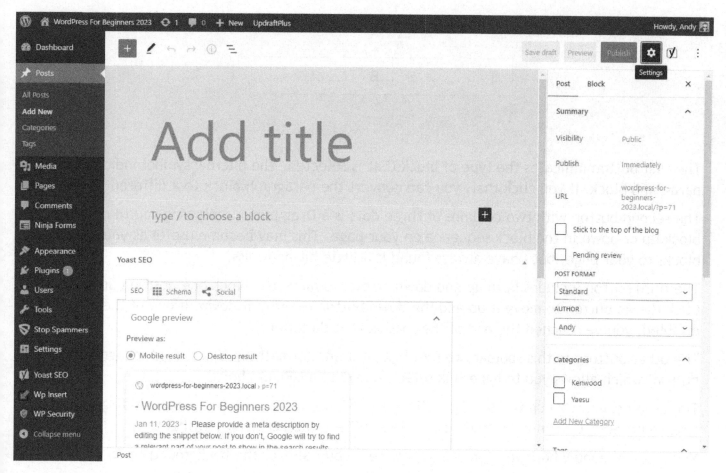

If you don't see the panel on the right, click the **settings** button. It looks like a cog.

There is a simple prompt: **Add title**.

Click into that box, and you can type the title of your post.

Under the title, you'll see this:

If you want to just add text, you can just click where it says **Type/to choose a block** and start typing. By default, this is a paragraph block. The + button on the right allows you to switch the block from a paragraph block to any other type of block you want to use.

However, if you just want to add some text below the heading, click on the block and start typing. Try it. Type a sentence of text and press the ENTER key on your keyboard. The editor will save that text as a paragraph block and create a new prompt underneath, which is the same prompt you saw above.

If you click somewhere inside the paragraph block you just created, a menu will appear above the block:

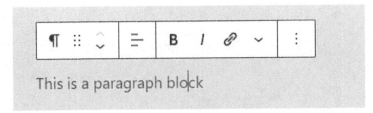

The first button indicates the type of block that is selected. The pilcrow symbol indicates a paragraph block. If you click that, you can convert the paragraph block to a different type.

The second button with two columns of three dots is a **Drag** button, allowing you to drag the block up or down in the block sequence on your page. This may become useful as you add more blocks to your page, but I have always found it a little hit-and-miss.

The third button includes both up and down arrows to move the block one position up or down. Click the up button to move it up and the down button to move it down. If one of these arrows is disabled, you've reached the end of the road in that direction.

The other buttons in this toolbar are for alignment and formatting. You should recognize the link button, which allows you to hyperlink selected text to a URL of choice.

The drop-down arrow on the far right offers a few more formatting options, including highlight text color. Select a sentence from your paragraph and then click on **Highlight**.

You'll see a menu where you can change the text color and/or the background color.

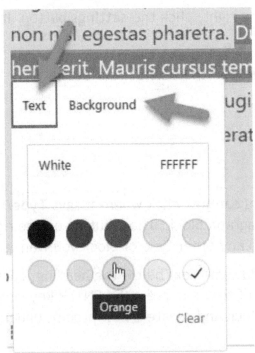

If you only want to change the color of the text, you can do that.

You will see a palette of recommended colors, but you can choose any color you want by clicking on the large rectangle showing the currently selected color (1):

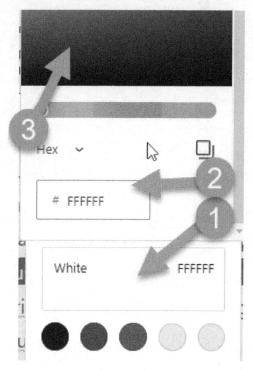

You can then choose from the spectrum display (3) or enter a hex value directly (2).

The final button in the toolbar is the **Options** button. This menu offers easy ways to add a new block before or after the current one and a few other useful features, including removing the block, duplicating the block, and creating a group including the selected block.

OK, let's add an image after the above paragraph block. When you pressed the **Enter** key after creating your first paragraph block, a new one was created underneath.

There are a few ways to add a specific type of block. The one I like the most is the / key on your keyboard. Click inside the new paragraph block and type a forward slash (/). A popup menu appears with the most common blocks:

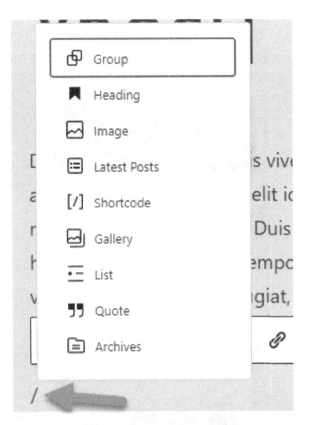

I can select an **Image** from that list, and the block will become an image block.

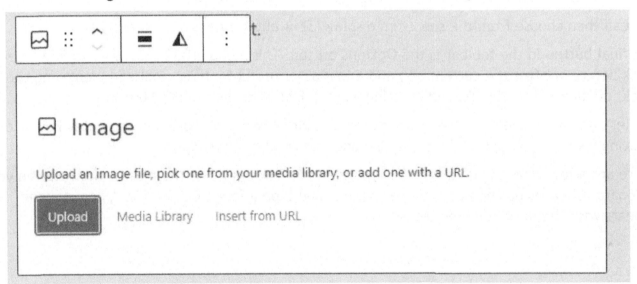

Notice that the toolbar menu on this block is a little different. This menu will change because it will only offer features that are compatible with the image block.

To insert an image, I can click **Upload** to choose one from my computer. During that upload, the image will be added automatically to the media library.

Another option is to click **Media Library** to open the library and add an image in the usual way.

The final option in that menu is to insert the image from a URL. This would mean the image is already on a web page somewhere. I should just remind you that images have copyright protection, so make sure you have permission to use images on other websites.

There is another option to insert an image. From your computer, drag and drop an image directly onto the image block.

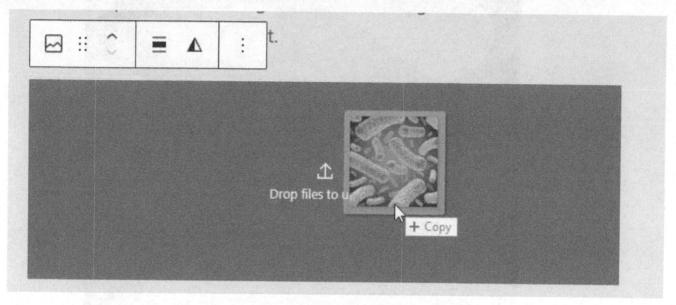

When you drop the image onto the block, it is uploaded to the media library and inserted into the image block.

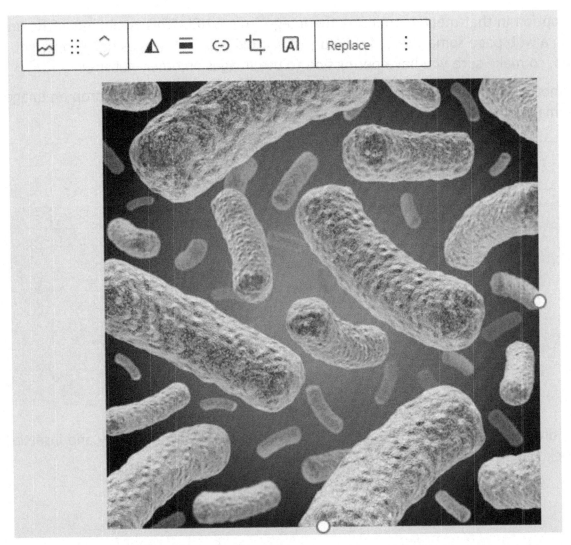

The menu on top of the image gives you a lot of options. Play with them to see what you can do.

Using the Forward Slash to Add Blocks

When you added a block by typing a forward slash (/), the popup showed common blocks. But what if the block you want to use is not in that popup? For example, what if I want to insert a video? If you check back, the video block was not in that popup.

Well, the solution is to type the / followed by the name of the block you want to use. e.g., if I type /v into the empty block, here is the popup:

Video is now on that list, and I can select it.

When you first start out with Gutenberg, you won't know what blocks are available. Therefore, I suggest you start off by clicking the + button in the top toolbar:

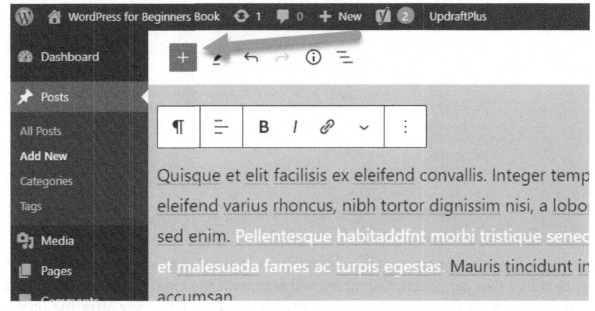

That will open a scrollable list of all blocks available:

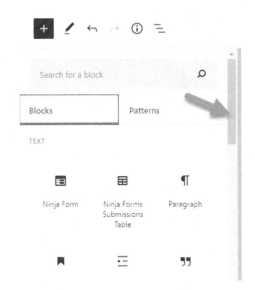

Go on. Open it and scroll down the list to see the range of blocks that are available to you. With Gutenberg, you build your web pages using these blocks.

In its simplest form, a post could be simply a title and a **paragraph** block like this:

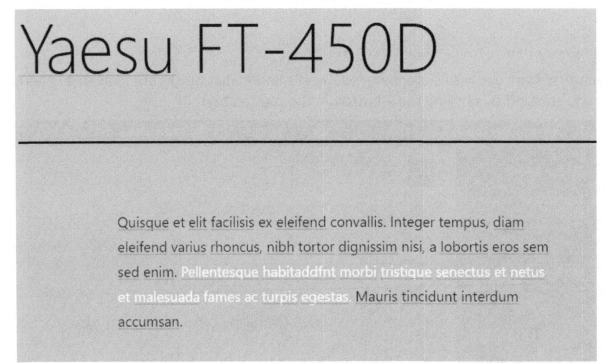

Note that there is only one paragraph per block. If you are writing a block of text and press the Enter key to start a new paragraph, Gutenberg will automatically create a new paragraph block for the second paragraph. In the following screenshot, I pressed the Enter key after the final word of the first paragraph:

Quisque et elit facilisis ex eleifend convallis. Integer tempus, diam eleifend varius rhoncus, nibh tortor dignissim nisi, a lobortis eros sem sed enim. Pellentesque habitaddfnt morbi tristique senectus et netus et malesuada fames ac turpis egestas. Mauris tincidunt interdum

¶ ⠿ ⌄ ☰ B *I* 🔗 ⌄ ⋮

Nulla porta ultricies pulvinar. Sed mollis ante id lorem finibus, in ultrices tortor dictum. Aenean consectetur orci quam, at porta arcu pellentesque sed.

Can you see that Gutenberg automatically created a new paragraph block? Go on and try it for yourself.

This auto-addition of new paragraph blocks makes writing long pieces of content very easy because you do not need to create paragraph blocks as you type manually.

If you tend to write your content in an external editor and then paste it into WordPress, you'll find that Gutenberg automatically splits the text into multiple paragraph blocks for you!

The advantage of using one block per paragraph is that each paragraph can then be formatted independently of the others.

Paragraph Block Properties

All blocks have their own properties. Since we've added a paragraph block, let's check out the properties because you can do some interesting stuff. Click into a paragraph block. On the right-hand side, you should see the **Block** tab has been selected:

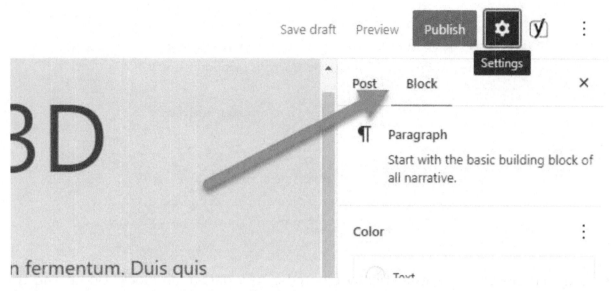

If you don't see the properties block at all, click on the small **Cog** button. You can see it in the screenshot above, right next to the **Publish** button.

The **Block** tab shows the settings for that block only (as opposed to the **Post** tab, which has settings affecting the entire post).

At the top of the paragraph block properties, you can select the text color and background.

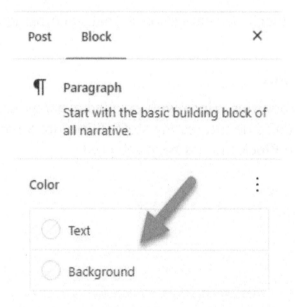

Don't be fooled into thinking these color options are disabled because of that icon. The icon simply means no color has been selected. Click on **Text** or **Background** to get a popup color picker.

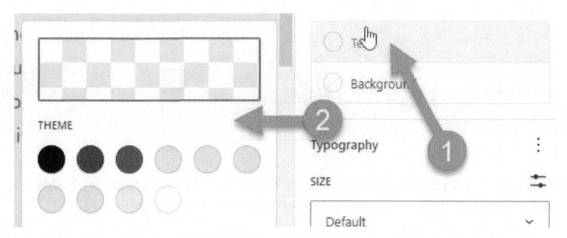

You can select a color from the palette or click on the large rectangle to choose from a color spectrum. If you are changing the background, you can even set up a color gradient.

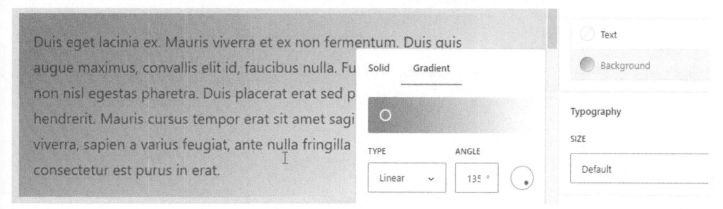

Under the color options, you can make changes to the text "typography." Click the size drop-down box to see a lot of options.:

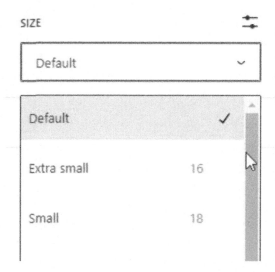

Either select a size from the **Font Size** drop-down box (try it!) or by typing in a custom size.

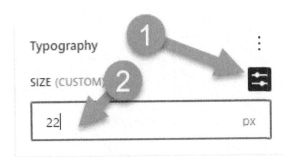

But size is just one of many attributes you can tinker with. A lot of options are hidden. Click the **Typography Options** button to see a full list of changes you can make:

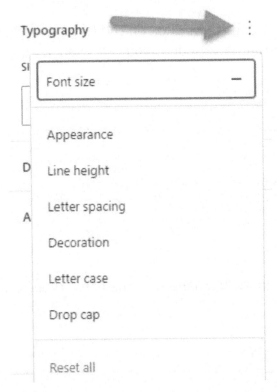

With that menu open, click each item to make them visible in the typography section. You'll end up with something like this:

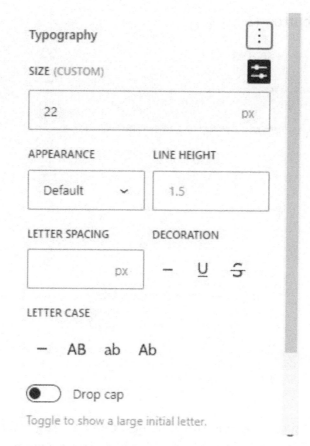

Play around with all those options to see what they do.

Under typography is a section called dimensions. Clicking the plus will open it out and allow you to select **Padding**. Padding is "white space" around your text.

By default, you'll see a horizontal bar that you can adjust by dragging the circle (1):

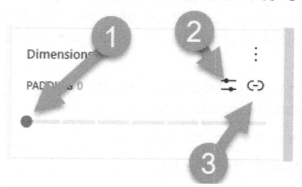

Drag that circle to the right and watch as the white space is added to the top, left, bottom, and right of your paragraph.

You have the option of providing a pixel value for the padding if you click the **Set custom size** button (2).

But what if you only want padding on the top, or bottom, or maybe left and right? You can do that

83

by clicking the **Unlink side** button (3).

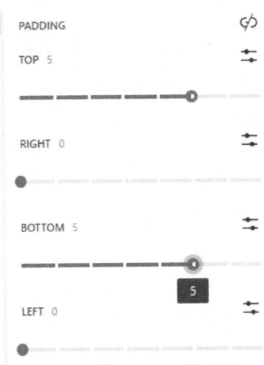

You now have sliders for each of the four sides, which can be dragged independently of each other. There is also a **Custom size** button if you want to specify pixel values for padding.

The final option in this block's properties is labeled **Advanced**. This allows you to assign custom CSS classes to the block (beyond the scope of this book) or add an HTML anchor. HTML anchors are available to most blocks, not just the paragraph. An HTML anchor is useful as it allows you to create hyperlinks that can jump from one part of the page to another. A good example of where you might want to use this is if you include a table of contents at the start of your article and you want to jump down to the relevant section of your article when the table entries are clicked. Let's try it.

Create 3 paragraph blocks on your post and fill each with a few sentences. A quick way to do this is to create one, then duplicate it a couple of times.

Click the final paragraph so you have access to the menu.

Open the **Options** menu and select **Insert before**.

A new block will be added right before the last paragraph. Click into that new block and type /h to bring up the block inserter popup and select **Heading**. Enter a short heading.

With the heading selected, the block properties now refer to that heading, so scroll down to **Advanced**. In the **HTML Anchor** box, type a word that is related to the heading. I'll call mine "summary."

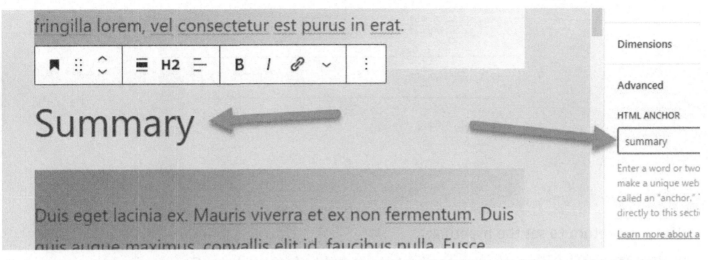

Now scroll to the first paragraph on the page and insert a block before it. Type something into the paragraph. Here is mine:

Highlight the word you want to use as the link to the HTML anchor you created and click the link button:

In the link popup, type a # sign followed by the word you entered for the HTML anchor without any spacing:

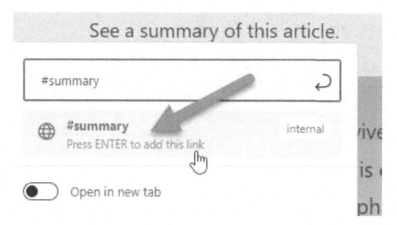

Now press return to set the hyperlink.

Publish or update your post using the button top right of your editor. Go and view your page using the **View Post** link, which will appear bottom left or is found in the sidebar on the right after publishing:

You'll see the link at the top of your post. Click it and watch your browser jump down to the heading. Cool, eh?

Now copy the URL in the address bar and look at it. It will be the URL of the page with the #anchor appended to the end, like this:

https://mydomain.com/yaesu-ft3d/#summary

If you paste that URL into a web browser, it will open with the anchor point at the top of the browser. That means you can use this URL on ANY page of your site to jump to this section of this article.

These are called jump links are useful.

The formatting options available for a block will obviously depend on the type of block you have selected, but the theme can also play a part. Some features, like full-width alignment, may be available for some blocks, but only if the theme supports it.

Before we leave this block, I wanted to mention a couple of items found in the **Options** menu. These items are found in the options menu of all blocks. The first one is the ability to turn a block into a reusable block:

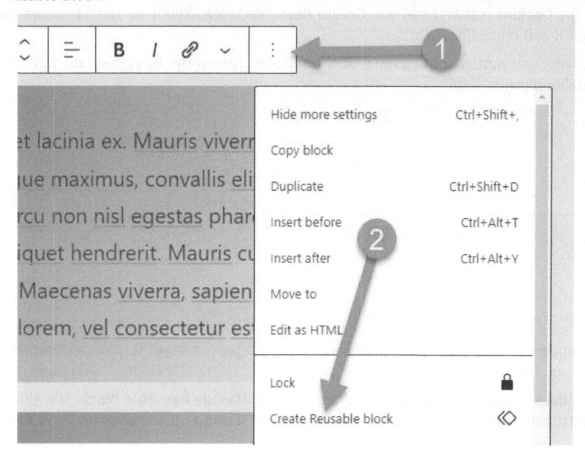

Let's see what that means.

Reusable Blocks

This is an interesting feature. It means you can create a block and save it so that it can be reused across your site on different posts and pages. If you update the reusable block, you update it everywhere you use it.

As an example, let's create a copyright notice and save it as a reusable block:

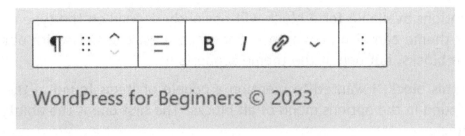

Clicking the **Options** button, I can now **Create Reusable block**. You'll be asked to name your block, so I'll call mine, Copyright.

Now click on the + button in the toolbar at the top and click on the **Reusable** tab. You'll see your new reusable block.

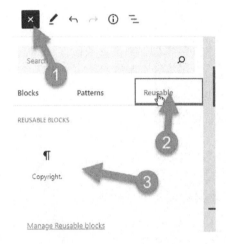

This will appear on this tab whenever you are creating a post or page, so you can insert it wherever you like.

When the date changes over to the next year, click the **Manage Reusable Blocks** link that you see at the bottom of that screenshot to be taken to a table showing all reusable blocks you've created.

You can click the edit link and change the year from 2023 to 2024. This change will be updated on every post and page where you've used this block.

What if I just wanted to edit the reusable block on one page without affecting it on other pages?

You can do that. When a reusable block is inserted into a post or page, select it to show the popup menu:

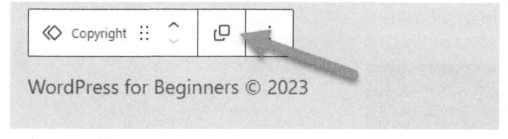

If your menu does not have the button shown with the arrow in the screenshot above, select the reusable block using the **List view**.

Click the **Convert to Regular Blocks** button.

Your reusable block on this page will be converted to a regular block that you can now edit without affecting the reusable block you saved or that reusable block on any other page of the site.

The final option in the paragraph's (and every other block) **Options** menu that I want to look at again is the **Group** feature. We have seen this already, but for completeness, I wanted to include it in the Gutenberg section of the book as well.

This creates a group of blocks that can be treated as a single entity. Once you've created your group, you can save it as a re-useable block if you want.

Create a new post, add a heading block, and type "Sign up for my newsletter."

Now add a paragraph underneath and type some text about how you "won't share details with other companies."

Now add a **Buttons** block (search using /b) underneath and change the label of the button to "Subscribe."

Here is mine:

Open the **List view** so you can see the three blocks you've added. SHIFT + click to select all three blocks. Now open the **Options for the Heading block** (though you can use the options menu of any of the selected blocks) in the **List view** and select **Group**:

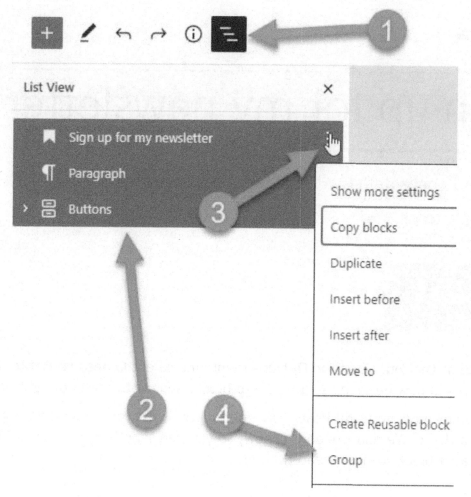

All three blocks are now added to the group, which you can select in the List View:

When you select the group in the list view, it becomes selected in the editor window:

Notice the menu at the top? Open the **Options** menu and select **Create reusable block**. Add a title. That group will now be saved as a reusable block along with the copyright notice.

Without saving your post, go to **All Posts.** Unless you published your "newsletter group" post, you should see it is a **draft**. We don't need this now, so you can send it to the trash. This will not delete the reusable block we just created.

Add a new post.

Click the + in the toolbar at the top, and select the **Reusable** tab. Add the newsletter block you just created.

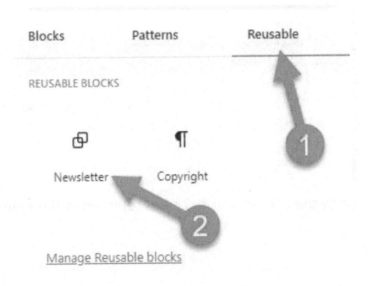

See how easy that was?

Groups have their own properties as well as the individual blocks that make up the group.

From the **List view**, select the **Group**. Be careful not to select the reusable block:

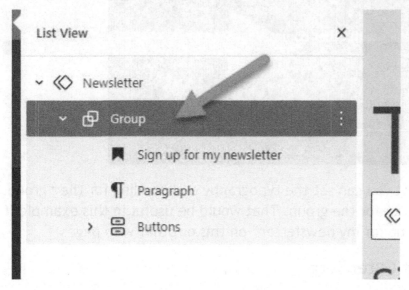

If the **Settings** pane isn't open, open it by clicking the cog. You will see that the group has its own properties.

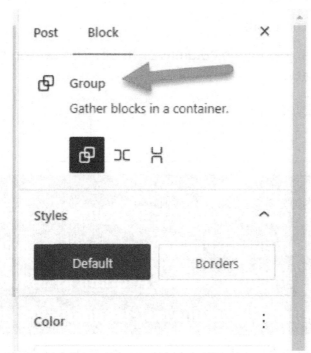

This means that all blocks inside the group can be manipulated as a single entity.

For example, by changing the background and font colors of the group:

You will also find that you can set the typography and padding for the "group." You can also specify an HTML anchor for the group. That would be useful in this example if I wanted to include sentences like "sign up for my newsletter" on this or other web pages.

Moving a Block in Gutenberg

Either open the post with several blocks or create a new post with several blocks.

Click inside the block you want to move.

Now, look at the buttons in the toolbar.

One of them has six dots arranged in two columns of three. This button allows you to drag and drop the block to the desired location:

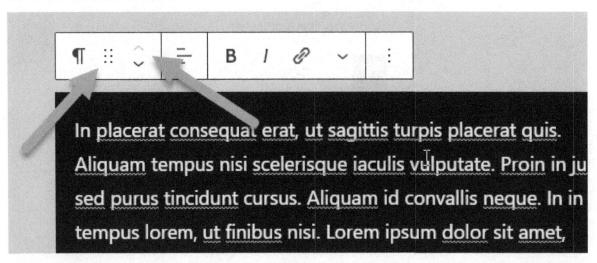

Just click and hold the mouse button down on this block. If you start to drag the block, it disappears, and you get a horizontal line that represents its position. Drag the line up or down to the desired location and drop:

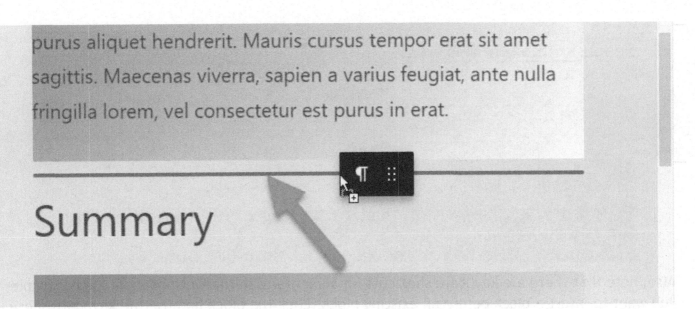

I find the drag-and-drop option is still quite fiddly, so I prefer the second option.

In the menu above the block you want to move are two arrows. One will move the block up one position, and the other will move the block down one position. This is my preferred method of moving blocks. Try it. Move a block up or down to see how this works.

Inserting Blocks in Between Existing Blocks

Each block in your post will display the toolbar at the top when you click on it. The right-hand button is the **Options** menu that gives you the opportunity to insert a block before or after the current one.

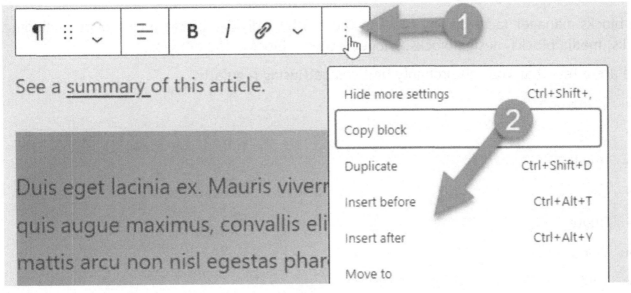

These options will insert a block which you can then work with:

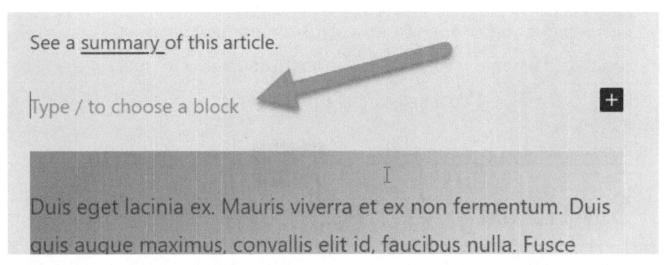

See a summary of this article.

Type / to choose a block

Duis eget lacinia ex. Mauris viverra et ex non fermentum. Duis quis augue maximus, convallis elit id, faucibus nulla. Fusce

Also, note that there are keyboard shortcuts for some items in the **Options** menu. For example, if you want to insert a block before an existing block, click the block and use the keyboard shortcut Ctrl+Alt+T (or the Mac equivalent). Ctrl + Alt + Y will insert after the current block.

Delete a Block

We have already seen this, but let's recap.

1. Select the block you want to remove.

2. From the **Options** menu, select **Remove "Block,"** or press SHIFT+ALT+Z on your keyboard.

So, we have the basics of adding, deleting, and moving blocks. But what blocks are available?

Available "Building" Blocks

The blocks manager (accessed by the + in the top left) divides blocks into groups, including text blocks, media blocks, design blocks, widgets, theme blocks, and embeds.

Here are a few that you will probably find yourself using regularly.

*   Paragraph
*   Image
*   Heading
*   List
*   Quote
*   Video
*   Table
*   Buttons

- Columns

- Spacer

I won't go through all the blocks that are available, as I want you to explore. It's easy. Create a post and add some blocks. Play with the settings in the block toolbar as well as the block properties in the right-hand pane.

There are three blocks I would like to look at briefly.

The Table Block

Creating a table used to be a chore when the Classic editor was the default WordPress editor. It meant having to create the table in HTML and insert it manually into the code of the post or page.

The table block in Gutenberg makes it very easy. You'll find it in the Text blocks section or by creating a new block and typing /t:

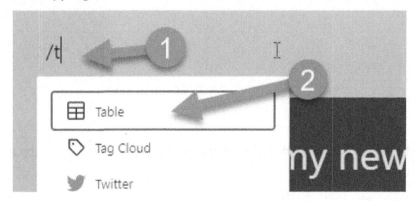

When you add a table block, you'll be asked for the row and column count. You can always edit this later by adding new columns or rows, but it is easier if you know now and can enter the precise dimensions.

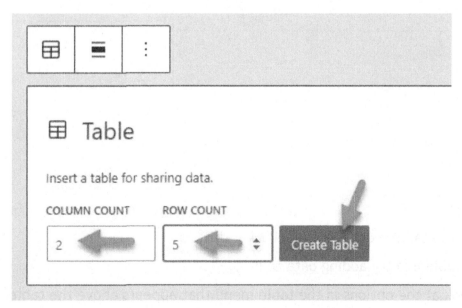

On clicking **Create Table**, you'll have a nicely formatted table awaiting data.

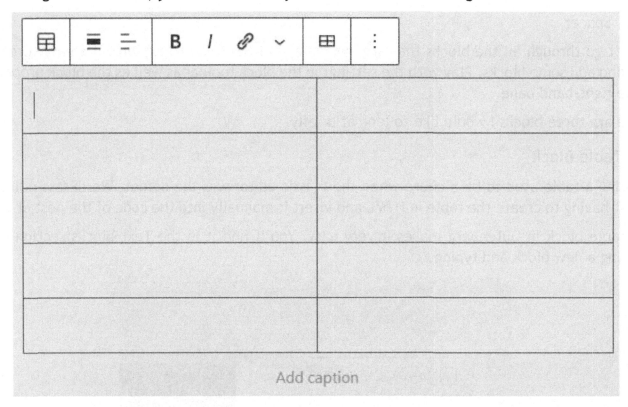

Notice the toolbar at the top. The **Edit Table** button gives you the power to add or delete cells:

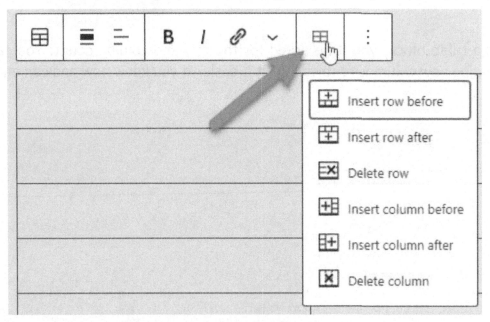

You can explore the table block for yourself. Try this:

1. Create a table and try adding data to it.

2. Have a look at the options in the table menu that appears above the table.

3. Try out the "styles" in the block properties panel.

4. Have a look at all the table block properties and work out what they do.

5. Insert additional columns and rows into the table.

6. Delete columns and rows.

The Buttons Block

Another cool block is the **Buttons** block. We saw it earlier when we created a newsletter sign-up reusable group.

When you add the button block, the caption of the button says **Add text...**

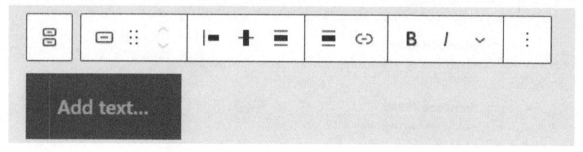

You can just click the "Add text" and start typing.

The buttons block allows you to create several buttons in a row.

Try this.

Add a buttons block.

Type a caption of the button and press the Return (Enter) key on your keyboard. Another button will be created:

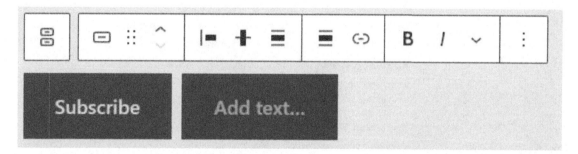

If you do this by accident, select the button you want to remove and use its **Options** menu to remove the button.

When a button is selected, you can use the **Link** button in the toolbar to specify a URL to visit when that button is clicked. Maybe the button is a buy button, and you need to link it to a PayPal URL.

Alternatively, you might want to link the button to an existing page on your site. Let's see how to do that.

Select the button and click on the **Link** button in the block's toolbar. Start typing in some text from the title of the post you want to link to, and it should pop up for you to select:

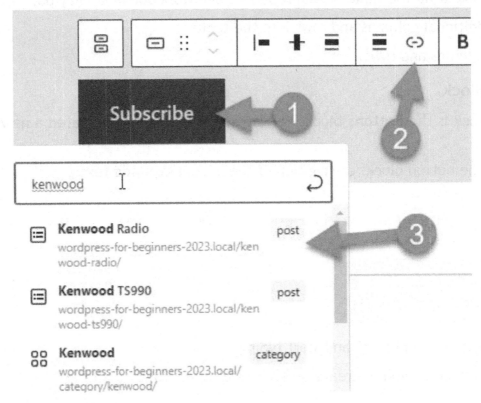

You can see that several posts matched my search, so I can click on the one I want to link to. If I want the button to open the post in a new browser tab, select that option first, then select the post.

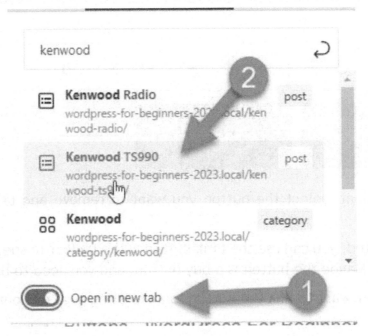

If you forget to set the post to open in a new window, you can fix this after the link is created. Simply click on the button, and a popup opens with that option available (1):

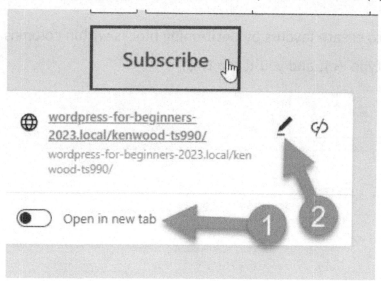

Also, notice the pencil icon (2), allowing you to change the link URL if needed, and the **Unlink** button next to it if you want to remove the link altogether.

Open the **List view** and you'll see that the button you added is a "buttons" block that contains your button. If you add another button, both buttons will be contained in that buttons block.

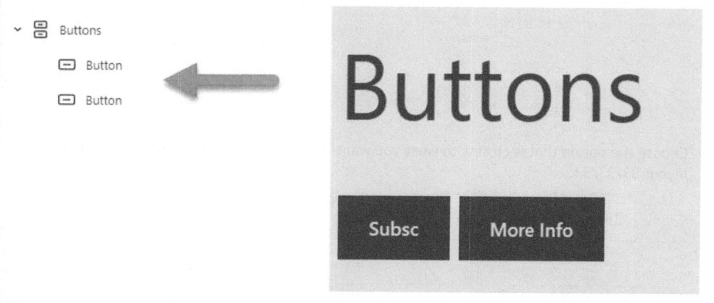

This is just a special type of group. As with the groups we have seen already, changing the properties of the **Buttons** block will change the properties of all buttons in the block. Suppose you want to change the properties of a single button. Select that button, not the buttons block.

Have a look at the block properties (right-hand pane) for both the Buttons block and individual buttons. You'll find an option for horizontal and vertical arrangement of the buttons in the block as well as some other familiar properties. Play around and see what you can do with this block.

The Columns Block

This block allows you to create layouts by positioning blocks within columns.

Add a columns block (type /c), and you'll see this:

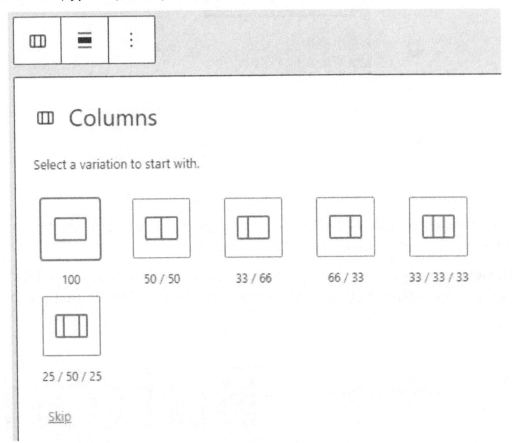

Choose the option that is closest to what you want to achieve. I'll choose the three-column layout 33/33/33:

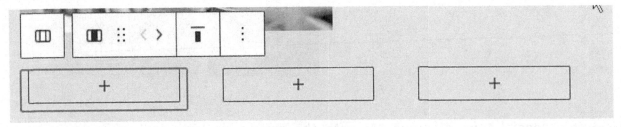

I can now add blocks to each of the three columns by clicking on the + symbol in the middle of the column. What makes columns so powerful is that you can add more than one block to each column. In the following screenshot, I have added an image to the first column.

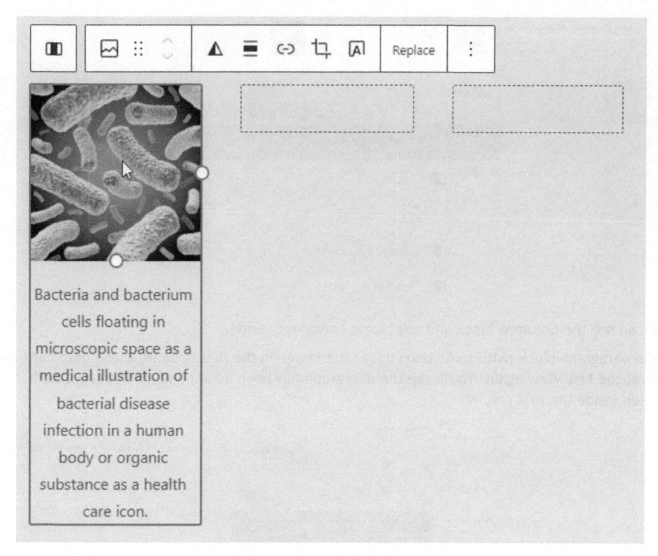

When I select that image, the menu changes to the "image menu."

I can insert another block above or below the image by using the image options menu. Alternatively, I can select the image and press the Return key on my keyboard to insert a new block underneath.

Select the **Columns** block from the **List View**:

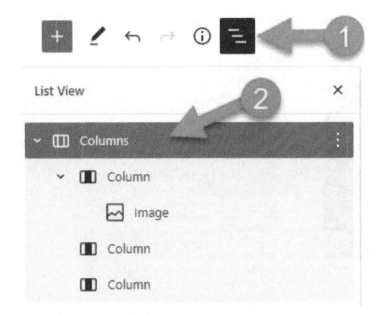

You can see the **Columns** block and any blocks contained inside.

Add a paragraph block (with some text) under the image in the first column, then come back and look at the **List View** again. You'll see the paragraph has been added under the image, both nestled inside the first column.

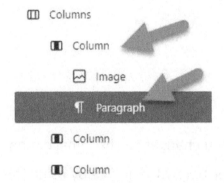

Select the **Columns** block from the **List View** to select the entire columns block. Now look at the properties panel to see the formatting options you have for the columns block:

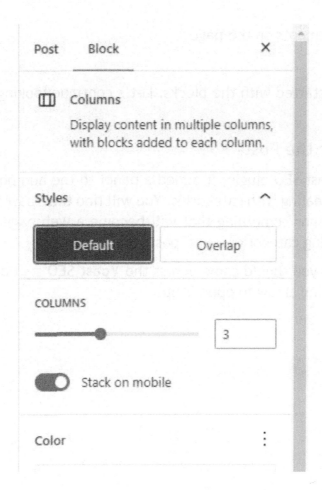

There are a couple of styles, but you can also change the number of columns:

The **Stack on mobile**, if enabled, will automatically stack the columns vertically when viewed on a mobile device for a cleaner look.

If an individual column is selected (use the **List View** button to select the second column), you get the properties for that specific column.

Have a play around with those settings. You won't break anything.

What happens if you select a block inside one of the columns?

The block properties panel will now show the properties for the selected block. The List view is a great tool for selecting elements on the page.

Oh. And columns are cool!

That's enough to get you started with the blocks. Let's continue looking at the other parts of the editor.

Yoast SEO Settings for the Post

When we installed the Yoast SEO plugin, it added a panel to the add post (and add page) screen. We saw this earlier when dealing with categories. You will find this Yoast SEO box of tricks wherever you are setting up or defining something that will become a web page on your site. That means when you are adding/editing categories, tags, posts, and pages.

If you scroll down a little, you should come across the **Yoast SEO** section. It may be collapsed, so click the little down-pointing arrow to open it up.

This Yoast SEO box looks like the ones we saw earlier. In this case, there are three tabs across the top. SEO, Schema, and Social.

The SEO Tab

At the top, we have the **Google Preview** section. We saw this when we looked at adding categories. Go back and refer to that section of the book as the same principles apply, just this time to posts.

The Cornerstone content feature is something I don't personally use in this plugin. If you want to learn more, click to open that section and visit the link:

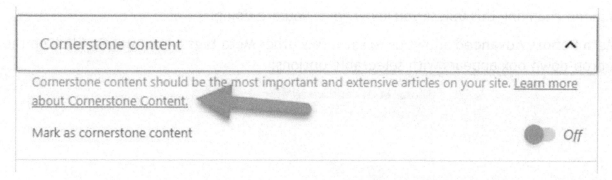

Some of the more powerful features of this plugin can be found in the **Advanced** section of the SEO tab. We covered it briefly when we looked at categories, but let's go over it again in a little more detail.

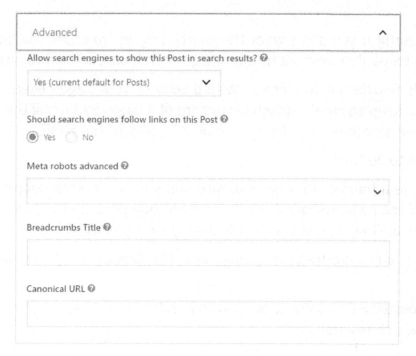

These settings give us fine control over how the search engines will deal with this post. We can use these settings to override the global settings for the site that are defined in the Yoast SEO sidebar menu we explored earlier. This is powerful. With this fine level of control, we can treat every post and page on our site differently if we want to.

The top setting allows us to show/hide a post from the search engines. By default, all posts will be indexed by search engines. If we don't want a post indexed and visible in the search engines, we can select **No** from the drop-down box (which sets the page to noindex and excludes it from the sitemap). However, this would be most unusual for posts. It's far more common to do this with pages, as we don't actually need legal pages or contact forms being indexed.

The next setting is whether search engines should follow links in this post. The default is yes, but we can set them to no (which is a nofollow tag for those that know what this means). I don't recommend changing this unless you know what you are doing.

The **Meta Robots Advanced** allows us to set a few other Meta tags on our pages. Click on the field, and a drop-down box appears with selectable options:

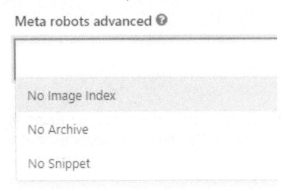

No Image Index is useful if you don't want the search engines to index the images on your page. Indexed images can be easily found within the image search on Google and pirated.

No Archive tag tells Google not to store a cached copy of your page. There are times when we don't want Google to keep an archive (cached version) of a page. By setting the post as **No Archive,** we are preventing the search engines from keeping a backup of the page.

Why might you want to do this?

Well, maybe you have a limited offer on your site and you don't want people seeing it after the offer has finished. If the page was archived, it is technically possible for someone to go in and see the last cached page at Google, which will still show your previous offer.

Breadcrumbs Title is a feature for those using Yoast SEO Breadcrumbs. These are not covered in this book.

No Snippet tells Google not to show a description under your Google listing (nor will it show a cached link in the search results).

The Schema Tab

Schema is a way of giving search engines more information about your content. In return, search engines like Google can create "rich" snippets in the search results that help your content stand out from the crowd:

www.bbcgoodfood.com › Recipes

Best ever chocolate brownies recipe - BBC Good Food

Ingredients. 185g unsalted butter. 185g best dark **chocolate**. 85g plain flour. 40g **cocoa** powder. 50g white **chocolate**. 50g milk **chocolate**. 3 large eggs. 275g golden caster sugar

★★★★★ Rating: 5 · 1,990 reviews · 1 hr · Calories: 150

The short version is that different types of web content can be marked up with different codes designed to provide information about that type of content.

The long version is that it is complicated and beyond the scope of this book.

While it is nice to know that Yoast SEO tries to help with schema, this plugin would only be scratching the surface in the way it helps implement schema. You can leave the default settings as they are.

The Social Tab

We saw this earlier in the book with categories. It allows you to specify an image, title, and description for Facebook and Twitter whenever anyone tries to share your webpage.

OK, that's it for the Yoast SEO box.

Post (Document) Properties

As you work on a post or page, you have access to the **Post** properties in the pane on the right:

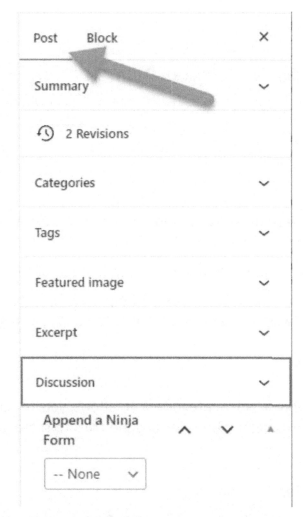

I have closed all the sections so I can fit them all in a single screenshot.

These settings allow you to set the category of a post, add tags, set a featured image, create an excerpt, etc. We typically use these settings as we prepare a post for publishing.

Let's go through the publishing process.

The Process for Publishing a Post

Once you have written your post, there are a few other things you may want to do before hitting the publish button. Let's look at the typical workflow:

1. Write a post.

2. Choose a category.

3. Add tags.

4. Insert featured image.

5. Add an excerpt.

6. Check/edit the slug of the post.

7. Publish or schedule.

I'll assume you have created your post and you want to go through and publish it. Let's go through the steps:

1. Choose category

From the Post properties, open the **Categories** section:

Select the desired category from the list, or **Add a New Category** if you want, directly from the Gutenberg editor.

2. Add tags

In the **Tags** section, add a list of comma-separated words and phrases you want to use as tags. When you type a comma, the editor will add whatever came before the comma as a tag.

3. Insert featured image

Featured images can be used by your theme, e.g., as an image next to each post on an archive page (e.g., Category, tag, etc.) or at the top of the post as a main image. Just click the **Set Featured Image** button to add an image from the media library (or upload). The recommended featured image size is different for every theme, so check your theme documentation to see what is recommended, but a fairly safe starting point is 1200x628 pixels.

4. Add an excerpt

Open the excerpt section and type in a paragraph about your post. This can be used by themes and/or plugins as a post summary, e.g., on recent post lists.

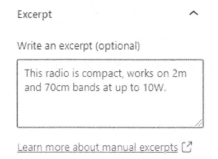

5. Check/edit the slug of the post.

WordPress creates the slug for a post based on the title you enter for that post. However, you have an option to manually edit the slug on a post-by-post basis. However, to edit this, you need to either publish the post or save it as a draft. The **Save draft** link is up there near the **Publish** button:

Save your post as a draft before continuing.

Then, in the **Summary** section of the post properties, click on the URL:

This will open a window showing the current slug, but you are free to edit this to whatever you want:

6. Publishing & Scheduling Posts

The top item in the post properties is **Summary**. These options allow us to publish and schedule content, as well as to choose the post format (we saw post formats earlier) and even send the post to trash.

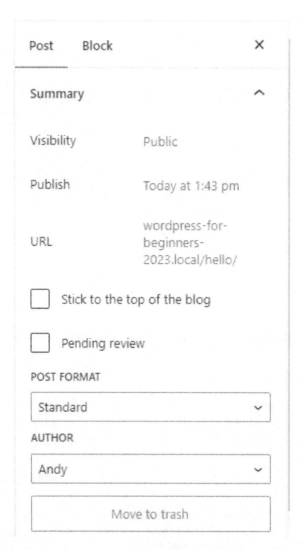

At the top, you'll see that the **Visibility** is set to **Public** by default. This means that once published, the post will be visible to anyone that comes to your site. If you click the **Public** link, you'll see that you can also set posts to **Private** or **Password Protected**.

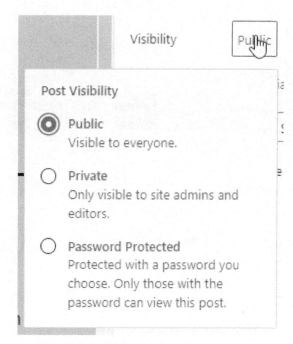

These are self-explanatory, so read the brief description of each.

Under the **Visibility** settings, you can see the **Publish** settings. With a new post, the default is "Immediately."

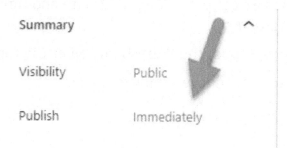

So once the post is published, it will go live on the site immediately. But you can click that **Immediately** link to get another option:

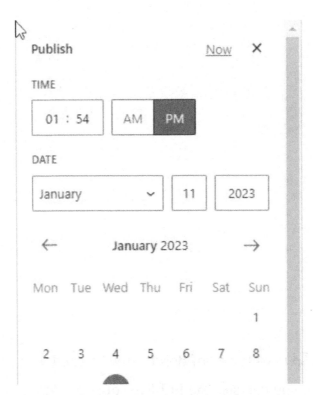

This popup calendar allows you to schedule the post's publication to a future date. Select a date and time in the future to schedule the post. When that date and time arrive, the post will be automatically published by WordPress.

If you do select a future date and time, the **Publish** button at the top will change to **Schedule.**

Click it, and you'll be asked to confirm everything is correct:

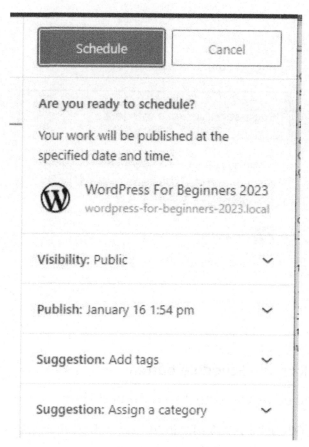

This screen offers a summary of the post and possibly suggestions as well. You can see the visibility and date to be published. In my case, it also suggests I add tags and assign a category. Clicking the down-pointing arrows next to these suggestions allows you to add these things directly in this screen:

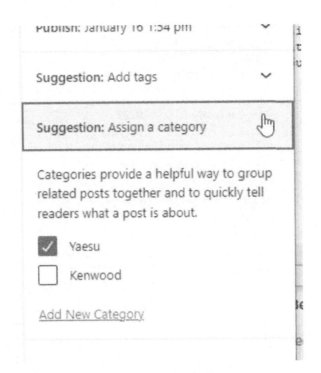

If everything looks OK, click on the **Schedule** button.

The post will then be published at the selected date and time.

In your **All Posts** screen, scheduled posts are given a "Scheduled" label, and you can see the date they are scheduled for:

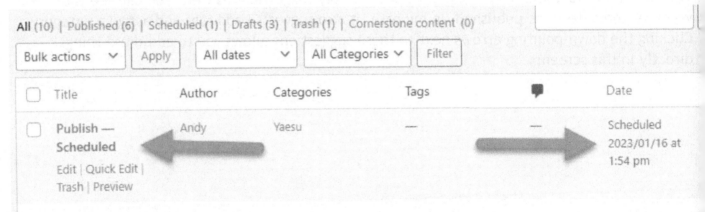

You'll also spot that new "scheduled" filter link at the top ;)

Using the HTML Editor to Edit Your Post

There may be times when you want to edit your post in raw HTML code. To do this, click on the **Options** menu button top right of the Gutenberg editor:

Currently, the **Visual Editor** is selected. It's what we have been using so far. If you choose **Code Editor** instead, you can view/edit the entire post as HTML code.

```
Yaesu FT3D
```

```
<!-- wp:paragraph -->

<p>See a <a href="#summary">summary </a>of this article.</p>

<!-- /wp:paragraph -->


<!-- wp:paragraph {"style":{"color":{"gradient":"linear-gradient(135deg,rgb(1,161,254) 0%,rgb(253,253,253)

100%)"},"typography":{"fontSize":"22px","textTransform":"none"},"spacing":{"padding":

{"top":"var:preset|spacing|60","right":"0","bottom":"var:preset|spacing|60","left":"0"}}}} -->

<p class="has-background" style="background:linear-gradient(135deg,rgb(1,161,254) 0%,rgb(253,253,253) 100%);padding-

top:var(--wp--preset--spacing--60);padding-right:0;padding-bottom:var(--wp--preset--spacing--60);padding-left:0;font-
```

You can make changes in the HTML editor and save changes as required. You can revert to the **Visual Editor** at any time by clicking that item in the same menu.

Editing Posts

At some point after writing a post, you may want to go in and edit or update it. This is an easy process. Just click on **All Posts** in the **Posts** menu. It will open a screen with a list of posts on your site.

Just click on the title of the post you want to edit, and it will open in the editor.

What if you had a lot of posts and needed to find one?

There are two ways of doing this. One is from within your Dashboard using the available search and filtering tools. The other method is one I'll show you later and involves visiting your site while you are logged into the Dashboard.

For now, let's look at three ways we can find posts from within the Dashboard.

Method 1: Perhaps the easiest way of all is to use the **Search Posts** feature. Type in a keyword phrase you know is in the title, and then click the **Search Posts** button.

The results will show only those posts that match:

Method 2: If you know what month you wrote the post, you could show all posts from that month by selecting the month from the **All Dates** drop-down box.

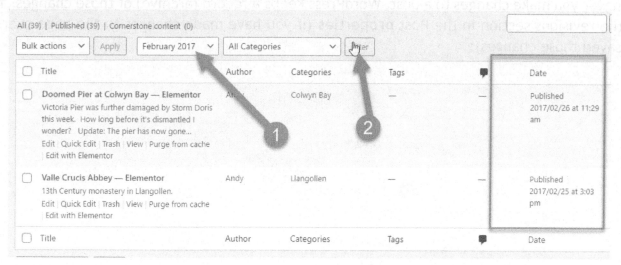

Once selected, click the **Filter** button.

Method 3: You can also search for a post by showing just those posts within a certain category. Select the desired category from the **All Category** drop-down box. Once selected, click the **Filter** button.

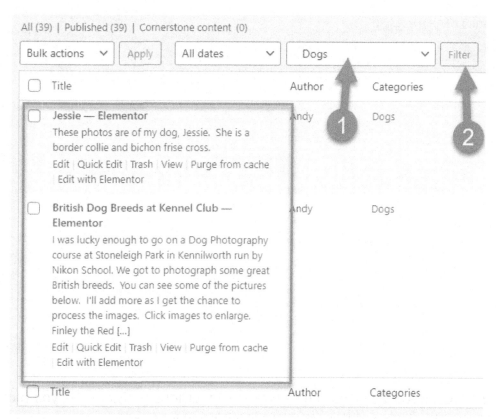

Revisions

Whenever you make changes to a post, WordPress keeps a record (archive) of those changes. You'll see the revisions section in the **Post properties** (if you have made changes to the page over time and saved those changes):

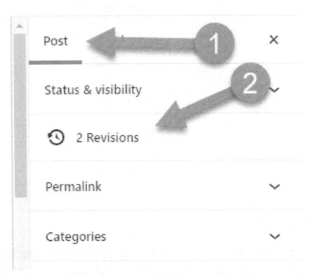

Click on the Revisions section to open it out:

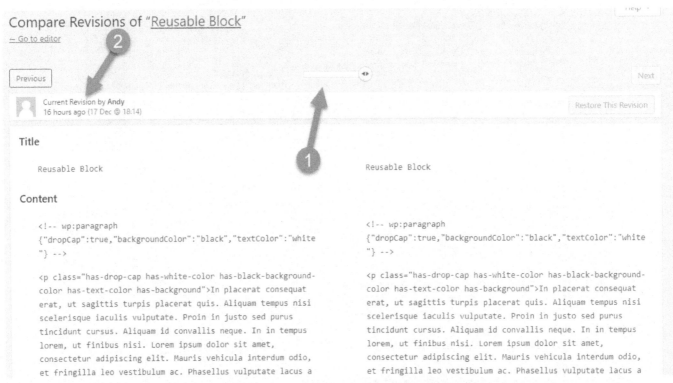

The slider at the top allows you to scroll between the various revisions. As you move through the revisions, you'll see the date and time that the revision was saved.

In the main window, you'll see the differences between the two revisions highlighted.

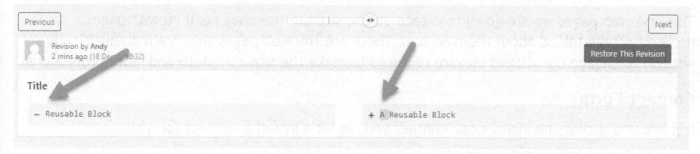

In the above example, I change the title from Reusable Block to A Reusable Block.

The latest version is on the right, and the previous version is on the left. As you scroll back through revisions, you'll always see two versions. On the right will be the version that was saved on that date. On the left was the previous version.

At any time, if you want to revert to a previous version, click the **Restore This Revision** button. The version on the right of the revisions screen will be the one restored. At the same time, a new revision is created for the "latest" version of the post.

Why Use Revisions?

Suppose you are working on a post and delete a paragraph or change an image. Later, you ask yourself, "why did I delete that?" With revisions, you can revert to previous versions of your post with a few mouse clicks.

Creating Pages – About, contact & terms

The first web pages we are going to create on the site are the ones I call "legal" pages. Remember? We talked about them earlier. These are the web pages that are not specifically written to engage our visitors but are required to make the site complete and more professional.

Contact Form

It's important that site visitors can contact you, so let's install a contact form plugin.

It's called Ninja Forms Contact Form.

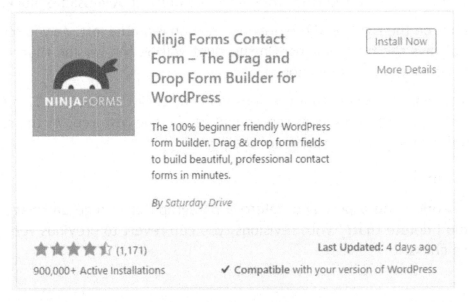

Install and activate the plugin.

This will add a new menu called **Ninja Forms** in the sidebar of the Dashboard.

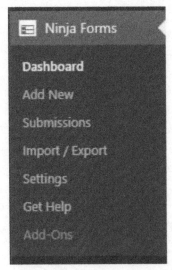

If you click on **Ninja Forms**, you'll be taken to the plugin's dashboard, where you can see that the plugin created a contact form for you.

We will use this one, as it is a perfectly good contact form. You just need to copy the **Shortcode**. You can see the shortcode in the table above. It's [ninja_form id=1].

Once you have copied it, create a new page by clicking on **Add New** in the **Pages** menu.

Add a title for the page, e.g., Contact Form, Contact, or Contact Us.

Now click where it says "Type / to choose a block":

Now paste in the shortcode. Publish your page.

You should get a popup in the bottom left of the screen after publishing.

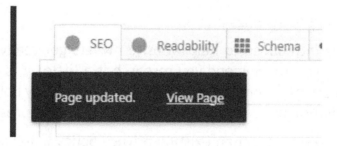

Click on **View Page** and your contact page with the form should appear.

About Us Page

OK, now for the "About Us" page. This is where you have a chance to write a little bit about yourself and your site so your visitors know about the person/company behind the site. The "About Us" page is often the most visited page on many websites, so bear that in mind.

Click **Add New** from the **Pages** sidebar menu.

This will start a new page.

For the title, use something simple, like "About," "About Me," or "About Us."

In the WYSIWYG editor, write the contents of your "About" page.

What should you include?

That is your choice, but here are some things I try to include in mine:

1. I like to begin by stating the goal of my website and usually approach this from the point of view of the visitors. What are their problems or interests, and how can my site help them?

2. Add your name and photo.

3. Add a bit of information about yourself.

4. Break up the page with bullet points and sub-headings to make it easier to read or scan.

5. Include your contact details or a link to your contact form. Note you can paste the contact form shortcode at the bottom of your about page to include it there as well if you want.

Once you have entered the text for your About page, click the **Publish** button to make it live on your site.

Visit your own about page.

You may find the comment form at the bottom of the page, so go in and turn it off if you need to.

Privacy Policy

Click on the **Privacy** link in the **Settings** menu.

The Privacy settings were introduced to help website owners get ready for GDPR compliance. If you don't know what that is, I recommend you research it a little. It is essentially a privacy law. One of the first steps in becoming compliant is to have a good privacy policy that visitors can read. This will tell them what information, if any, your site collects and stores.

The Privacy options allow you to select an existing privacy policy if you already have one or create a new one.

When you installed WordPress, a draft Privacy Policy was created for you. Head on over to the

Pages, All Pages screen, and you'll see it listed:

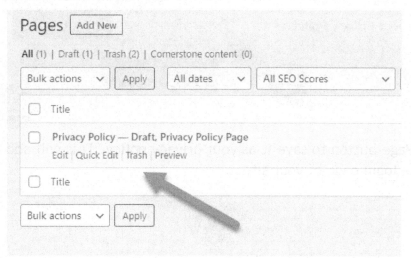

Go in and edit the draft page:

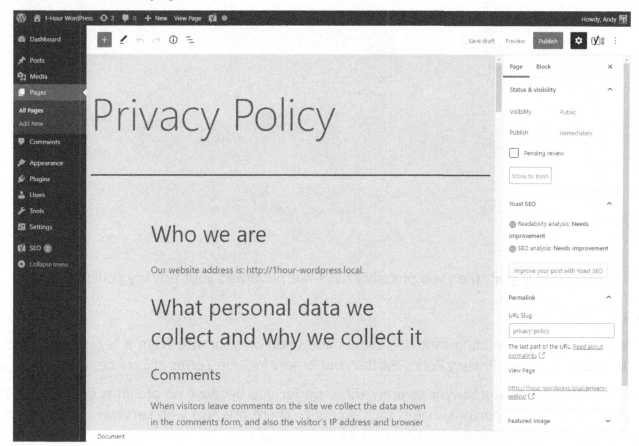

WordPress will include essential information relating to WordPress itself, but you will need to go through the policy and flesh it out. Once it is complete, publish the policy.

Now go back to the Settings, Privacy screen. Make sure your new privacy policy is selected:

Click the **Use This Page** button to save it as your privacy policy. This will add a link to your privacy policy on the login page of your site:

If you don't see that link, then you probably have not published your privacy policy.

Terms & Disclaimer

The legal pages are the important documents you need on your site from a legal point of view. We've already seen the Privacy Policy earlier, but others include Terms of Service, Disclaimer, etc.

Ideally, you would want a lawyer to draw these up for you because no plugin is going to be 100% complete or take your personal needs into account. There are also web services out there where you can buy packs of legal documents you can update and use.

So, with that said, be aware that while I will show you a plugin to add these to your site, it is only to get you up and running quickly. I'd still recommend you get proper legal documents drawn up.

There are a few plugins out there that can create quick legal pages. The one I suggest you look at is called WP-Insert.

Install and activate it.

You'll find a new menu in the sidebar navigation labeled **Wp Insert**. Click on it to open the settings.

Now, this plugin does a lot more than just generate legal pages. It's also a full-blown ad manager, which is useful if you want to put adverts or AdSense on your site.

For legal pages, we need to scroll down to the "Legal Pages" section:

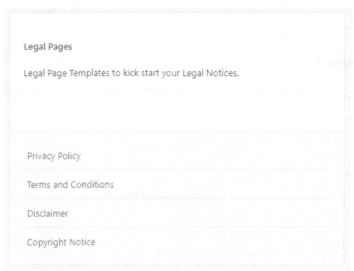

You can see that this plugin can create a Privacy Policy (which you should have created earlier, so you probably don't need), Terms and Conditions, Disclaimer, and Copyright Notice. You create all these pages in the same way, so I'll just go through one with you.

Click on the **Terms and Conditions** link.

A dialogue box pops up with the information you need to read.

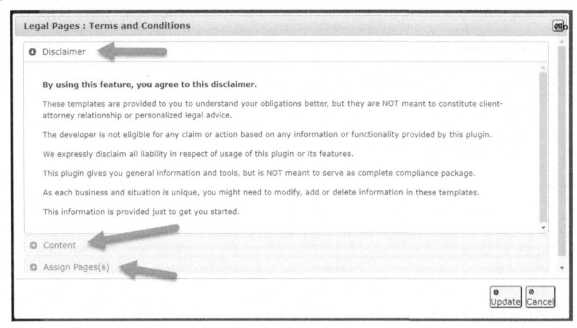

Notice that the plugin recommends you get proper legal advice for this type of document. That echoes the advice I gave you earlier.

Note the three tabs on the left: Disclaimer, Content, and Assign Page(s).

Click on the **Content** tab. You will see the default content of the Terms and Conditions page. You can edit this if you want.

Now click on the **Assign Page(s)** tab.

Click the **Click to Generate** button.

The plugin will create a page for the document. Once done, you can see it selected in the **Assign a Page** box:

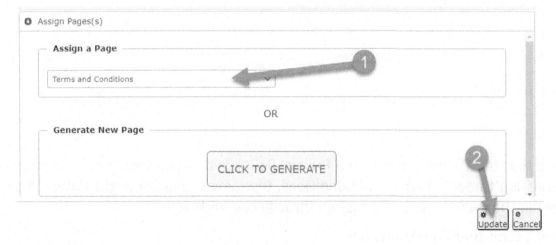

To confirm this is correct, click the **Update** button.

If you click on the **Pages** link in the sidebar navigation to view all of your pages, you will now find the Terms and Conditions page.

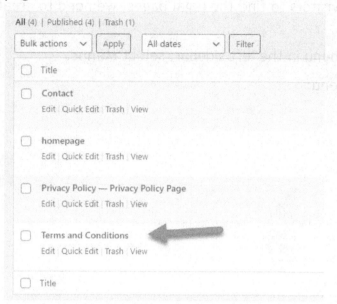

Click on the **View** link to open the page in your web browser.

Note that if you go in to edit this page, it will be blank. The plugin will create this page when it is requested by a visitor, so you need to keep this plugin active after you've created the legal pages.

Repeat for other legal documents you want to create.

Top Navigation Menu

To make it easy for site visitors to find the legal pages, we need to create a custom menu. Let's do that now.

Under the **Appearance** menu in the left sidebar, select **Menus**.

Enter a name for your menu:

I call this menu my **Legal**. Always give menus a descriptive name so you know what they are simply by looking at the title.

Check the box **Primary Menu**, and click the **Create Menu** button. This creates an empty menu and sets it as the site's primary menu (under the header at the top of the page).

Note: Every theme is different, so if you don't see the same **Display locations** as I have in the screenshot, check the documentation that came with your theme and choose the location that represents the top, underneath the header.

On the left, you'll see a list of your pages. There are three tabs to this selector – Most Recent, View All, and Search. If you don't see the pages you want to add, click on the View All tab:

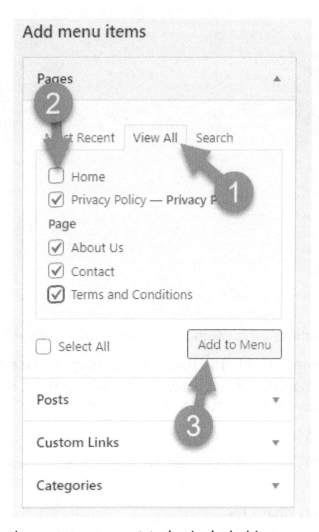

Place a checkmark next to the pages you want to be included in your menu. I've checked:

- Privacy Policy

- About Us

- Contact

- Terms and Conditions

This menu will link to all the important pages.

Once checked, click the **Add to Menu** button.

You will now see your list of pages in a column on the right. You can click and drag these pages on the right to re-order them.

You can also nest menu items like this:

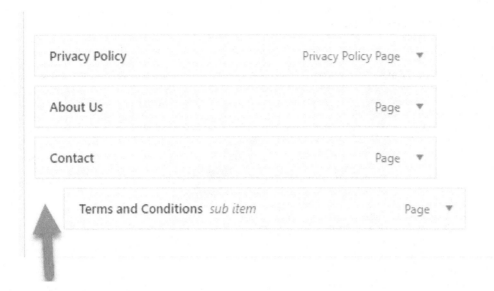

See how the Terms and Conditions item is indented under the "parent" Contact page?

When you indent pages in a menu, only the parent pages show in the menu on your site, but when a visitor moves their mouse over the parent page, a drop-down menu appears showing the indented pages. Click the **Save Menu** button to save your work.

Try it and see what happens by visiting your site.

To remove the indent, simply drag the indented item back flush to the left margin with the other items. Then **Save Menu.**

If I check my site now, this is what I see:

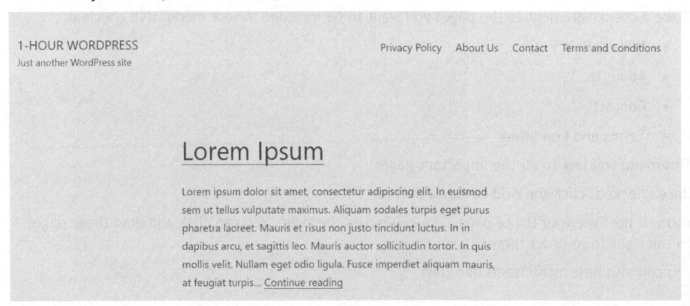

The only thing I will change is the text used in the menu items. I'd like Privacy instead of Privacy

Policy and Terms instead of Terms and Conditions.

Go back to the Appearance, Menus screen, and click the little arrow to the right of Privacy Policy:

Now edit the **Navigation Label** to your desired text.

Repeat for any other labels you want to edit, and then click the **Save Menu** button.

Finally, if you want to re-order the items in the menu, drag and drop them into the correct order and **Save** the menu again.

Here is my completed menu on the site:

A Note About Menu Locations

When designers are creating WordPress themes, they design them with menu locations in mind. Most themes will allow a menu at the top of the page, usually under the main site logo (Primary Menu in the Twenty Twenty-One theme), but some themes will have multiple locations designed for menus.

In the Twenty Twenty theme, there are five possible locations where you can put a menu.

Menu Settings

Auto add pages	☐ Automatically add new top-level pages to this menu
Display location	☑ Desktop Horizontal Menu
	☐ Desktop Expanded Menu
	☐ Mobile Menu
	☐ Footer Menu
	☐ Social Menu

Every theme is different, so you will need to check the theme documentation to see where each menu location is on your web page. Of course, you could just insert a menu at each location and visit your site to see where they end up.

However, on some themes, there will be special menu locations, e.g., "social menu" and "mobile menu," which may have special requirements and functions, so ultimately, you may need to read that documentation.

Since different themes offer different options for menu locations, if you decide to change to a different WordPress theme later, you may have to re-arrange your menu(s).

While menu locations allow easy insertion of menus, you can also add menus to other locations using widgets. For example, I used to add a menu to the sidebar of a site, and that requires a widget. We'll look at widgets later.

Creating Categories

OK, so the site is starting to take shape, but we need to start adding the content that we want our visitors to read. This is where we start adding posts. Before we do that, we need to set up some categories, which will be the filing system for these posts.

Setting up the Categories

I always like to start by creating the first few categories for the posts I know I want to write. You can create categories on the fly as you need them. However, since I have already planned my site, I know three categories I will be using. Remember this:

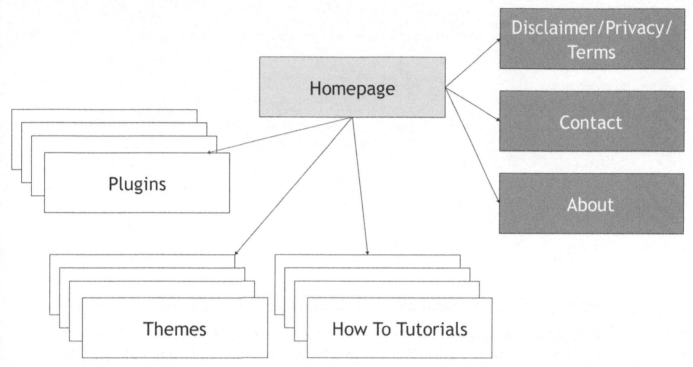

So, I have categories for:

1. Plugins

2. Themes

3. Tutorials

Let's set up those categories now. They won't appear on the site until a post is added to the category, so you don't end up with empty categories.

Click **Categories** under the **Posts** menu in the left sidebar.

On the right of the categories screen, you can see a list of all existing categories. The only one you have now is **Uncategorized.** This is the one that WordPress set up to be used as a default category. If you enter a post and forget to select a category, WordPress will choose this one by default.

I want my "tutorials" category to be the default category. The easiest way to do this is to edit the "Uncategorized" category.

Click the **Edit** link under the **Uncategorized** category.

You can now edit this category:

Edit Category

Name	Uncategorized
	The name is how it appears on your site.
Slug	uncategorized
	The "slug" is the URL-friendly version of the name. It is usually all lowercase and contains only letters, numbers, and hyphens.
Parent Category	None ∨
	Categories, unlike tags, can have a hierarchy. You might have a Jazz category, and under that have children categories for Bebop and Big Band. Totally optional.
Description	Add Media Visual Text
	Paragraph ▾ B I ☰ ☰ ❝ ☰ ☰ ☰ ⌘ ☰ ✕ ▦

Enter the name of your chosen default category. In my case, it's "tutorials."

Delete the contents of the **Slug** box, and leave it empty. The slug is the text that will be used in the URL of posts for the category part. If the slug is blank when you save your category, WordPress will use the category name to create a slug, with spaces being replaced by dashes.

Note that you can enter a slug when creating your categories. This can be useful if you want the slug to be different from the category name.

Leave the **Parent** box as **None**. Choosing a parent allows you to nest categories in much the same way we did with menu items when constructing the legal menu. I don't want nested categories, so no "Parent."

In the description box, enter a few sentences to describe the purpose of the category.

When you have finished, click the **Update** button.

If you go back and look at your list of categories (Posts, Categories menu), your new default category will be listed in place of the old "Uncategorized" category:

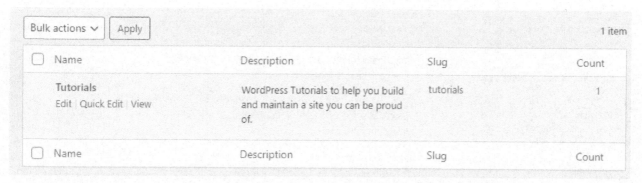

Note the "Slug" column. WordPress has given my "tutorials" category the slug "tutorials." That is, the same as the category name. This will now create URLs that look like this:

https://1hour-wordpress.local/tutorials/using-an-image-for-the-logo

To enter new categories, just add the information on the left side of the **Categories** page and click the **Add New Category** button when done:

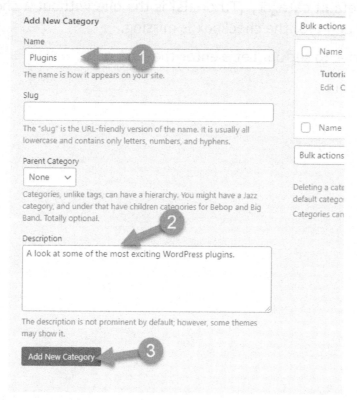

Here is my final list of three categories.

	Name	Description	Slug	Count
☐	**Themes** Edit | Quick Edit | Delete | View	WordPress themes are like skins. They give your site its look and feel.	themes	0
☐	**Plugins** Edit | Quick Edit | Delete | View	A look at some of the most exciting WordPress plugins.	plugins	0
	Tutorials Edit | Quick Edit | View	WordPress Tutorials to help you build and maintain a site you can be proud of.	tutorials	1
☐	Name	Description	Slug	Count

I'll add more as and when I need them.

You'll notice that the default category (Tutorials) is the one without a checkbox next to it. Since this category cannot be deleted, the checkbox is missing.

OK, I've got the categories to set up. Let's enter the first post.

Creating Posts Workflow

Let's create a workflow for entering a post that you can follow every time you want to create a new article on your site.

1. Create a new, blank post.

To do this, select **Add New** from the **Posts** menu in the left sidebar.

You now have a blank post ready for entry.

2. Enter a title

Make sure the title tells the visitor what the post is about without being overly long. For my first post, I'll call it:

"Recommended Web Hosts and Registrars"

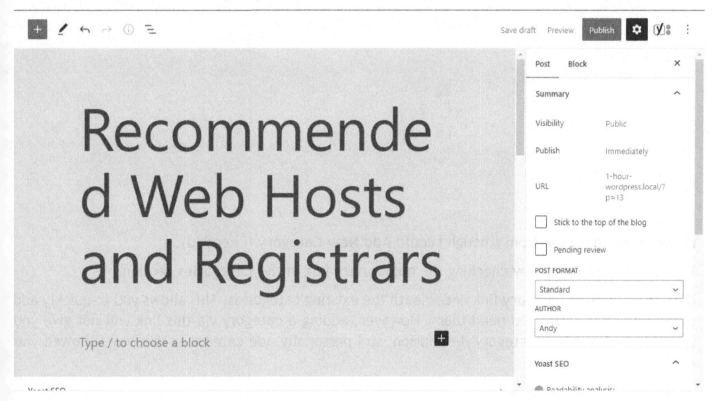

This will be a post about recommended web hosting companies and registrars.

3. Type in the post content

You can type your content directly into the Gutenberg editor. However, some people prefer to write their content in Microsoft Word first and then copy it across to WordPress. With the Gutenberg editor, simply copy the Word document and paste it into the main "Start writing or type/choose a block" window. You should find your formatting is largely preserved.

4. Select a category

Once the post is complete, choose a category. Make sure you are on the **Post** properties tab:

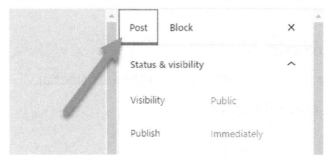

All of the document properties are found in the right-hand sidebar. You'll find an expandable section called **Categories**. Click anywhere in the category "bar" or the downward pointing arrow to expand that section:

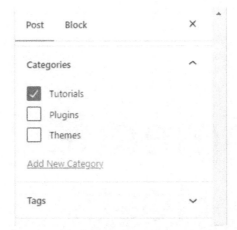

I have three to choose from (though I could **Add New Category** if needed).

You select the category by checking the appropriate box in the **Categories** section.

Note the **Add New Category** link underneath the existing categories. This allows you to quickly add other categories when you need them. However, adding a category via this link will not give you the option of adding a category description, so I personally add categories the way I showed you earlier.

5. Do you need tags?

Since this is my first post, I won't be adding any tags. As I add more posts to the site, I will consider whether they are needed. It is easy enough to go back in and add them to posts, so you don't have to do everything at the time of publishing.

Adding tags is as simple as typing them into the **Tags** section of the document properties. Separate multiple tags with commas (or the Enter key), and WordPress will handle the rest.

6. Add an Excerpt

We talked about excerpts earlier in the book. I recommend you add an excerpt for all posts on your site.

Enter a two or three-sentence summary of the post in the **Excerpt** section of the document properties. Your visitors will probably read this excerpt as a description of the post on certain pages of your site. Therefore, try to get in their heads and figure out what would make them click through to read the post. Enter that as the excerpt.

7. Featured Images

Featured images can be used by your theme to display a small thumbnail image next to the title and excerpt of your post in, for example, a list of related posts. If you want to add one, then you do so in the **Featured Image** section of the document properties. The exact dimensions of the featured image can vary between themes, so check that documentation. As a general guideline, create a 1200 x 600 image and upload that as your featured image. WordPress will resize it accordingly.

8. Publish the post

Click the **Publish** button. You can then choose when and how you want to publish:

When you are happy with your selections, click the **Publish** button again to make the post live on your site.

What to do next?

You can now go off and start writing posts on your website. However, as you do, keep an eye on what is happening with your website. By default, the latest posts are displayed on your homepage, with the last published post at the top. If you prefer to have a more "static" homepage without displaying my latest posts like that, I'll show you how to do that soon.

In the next chapter, I want to have a look at widgets. We mentioned them earlier and saw them in the footer section of our web pages.

Widgets

Widgets allow you to easily add visual and interactive components to your site without needing any technical knowledge. It's one of the things that makes WordPress so powerful.

If you want to add a list of your latest posts, there's a widget for that. Perhaps you want to add a poll to your site? That can be done with widgets too. There are some widgets specifically designed for these (and other) purposes, but you can also create your own using any of the blocks built into Gutenberg.

When a designer creates a WordPress theme, their initial drawing will probably have "widgetized" blocks drawn onto it so they can visualize which areas will accept widgets. Maybe it will look something like this (with the shaded areas able to accept the widgets):

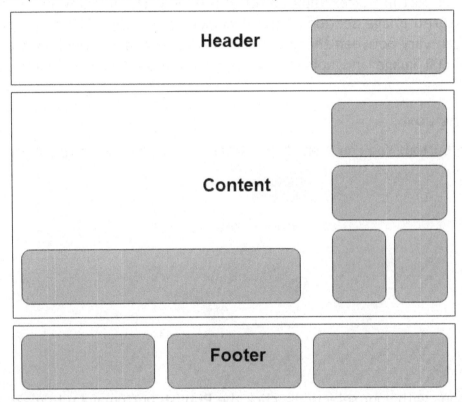

The usual areas that accept widgets are the header, sidebars, and footer. Sometimes you can also add widgets after post content.

With the Twenty Twenty-One theme, we have already seen that the only widgetized area is the Footer. Other themes may have different areas for widgets.

Let's have a play around with widgets. Click **Widgets** in the menu to be taken to the widgets screen.

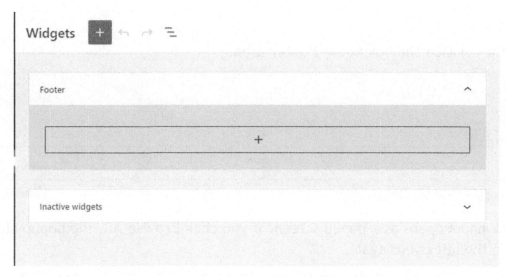

We saw this screen earlier, so there is no need to go over the interface again. Let's just try out a few widgets.

Click on the **Add Block** button in the toolbar.

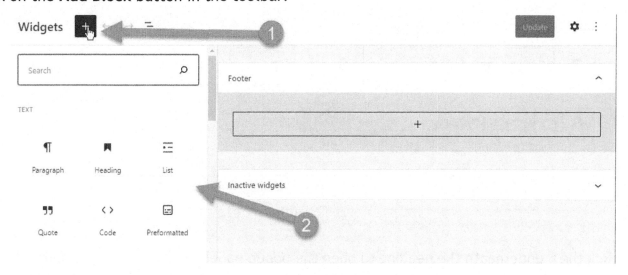

The panel on the left opens to show you available blocks and widgets you can insert.

The blocks are divided into related groups, so you have text blocks, media blocks, etc. These are the same blocks that are available to you as you create your posts or pages. At the top is a search box, so you can easily search for the widget you want to insert if you know what it's called.

You will also see a group called **Widgets**. These are blocks that have been created specifically to be used as a widget, and they have specific functions.

For example, the **Latest Posts** widget will add a list of the most recent posts on your site. The **Navigation Menu** widget will insert one of the menus you created into the widget areas, and so on. The **Search** widget will insert a search box, and so on.

Close the block inserter panel on the left by clicking the X that replaced the + button when you opened the panel.

Now click on the + inside the box in the **Footer** area:

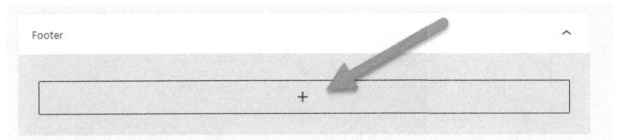

A smaller block panel opens as a popup screen. If you click **Browse All**, the popup closes, and the larger panel on the left opens again.

Open the popup panel again and click on the **Heading** block in the block panel. This will insert that block into the **Footer**. Give it the title **Welcome** and make it Heading 2 by using the formatting menu above the Heading block.

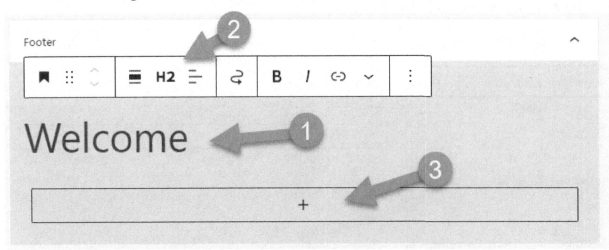

Now click the + underneath the heading to open the popup panel again and add a paragraph block. Add something like:

"We hope you find what you are looking for, but if not, please use the search button below:"

Now click the + underneath the paragraph block and insert that search widget we saw earlier. Hint: You can find it by browsing all blocks or by using the search feature built into the popup panel.

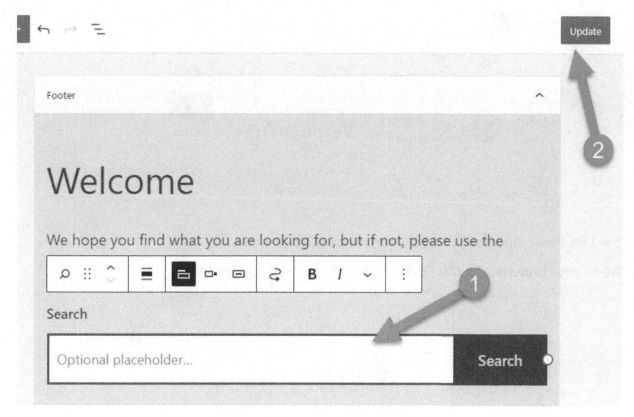

Now click the **Update** button to save your widget area.

If you now visit your site, you should see your new content in the footer widget area:

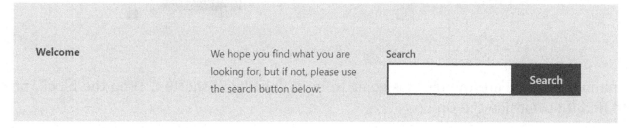

Hmmm. That's not exactly what I wanted. I'd prefer the title to be on top of the paragraph and the search box underneath. The good news is that it's easy to fix using **Groups**.

Go back to the **Widgets** screen and click the + to open the block inserter.

Find the **Group** block and drag one over the footer area and drop it.

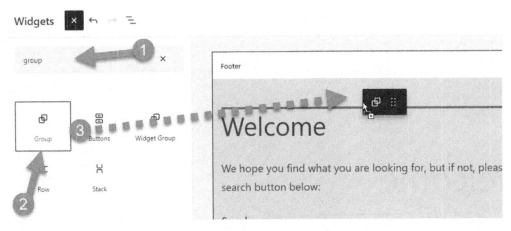

Open the List View, and you'll see the new Group block added.

Drag the header underneath the **Group** and slightly over to the right.

The line indicating where the block is going to be dropped will shorten. Drop the block, and you should find it now inside the Group.

Repeat for the paragraph and search blocks.

When all three are inside the group, re-order them as necessary by dragging them up or down, or clicking on the blocks in the editor area and using the up/down arrows.

The three blocks have now been grouped into a single widget. You can see this by clicking on the **List View** button:

See how the three blocks are now indented under the **Group**?

Click **Update** to save your widget settings, and go back and visit your homepage.

The blocks in the group are now stacked vertically.

If you knew this was how you wanted these blocks to appear in the first place, you could have added the Group block first, then added these directly inside the Group.

Have a play around with widgets until you are happy manipulating the blocks and grouping them.

The Homepage - A special case

By default, WordPress will show your recent posts on the homepage. I personally don't like this and prefer total control over what is displayed on my homepage. In fact, I create a page of content to use for my homepage and show that instead of a list of posts. This is easy in WordPress. We simply set up the homepage to show a "static" page.

The first step in achieving this is to create a new WordPress page to use as our Homepage.

Go and click on the **Add New** item in the **Pages** sidebar menu.

Give your page a title that will be displayed at the top of your homepage.

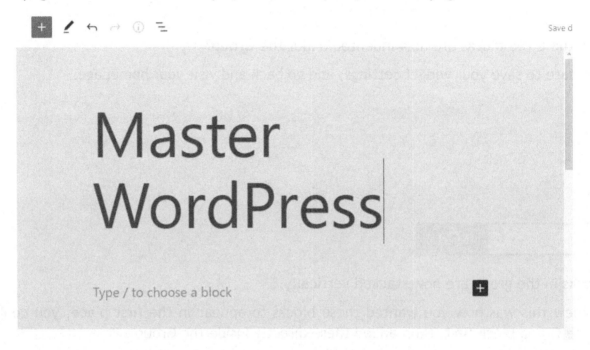

Add the content you want to be displayed on your homepage using Gutenberg blocks.

After publishing the page, your homepage will still look the same. It still lists the most recent posts.

Don't panic. That's simply because we have not told WordPress to use the new page as a homepage.

To do that, go to the **Reading** settings inside the **Settings** menu in the left sidebar.

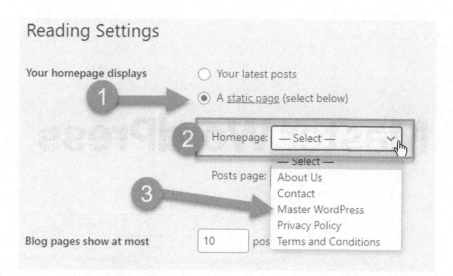

Select **A static page** from the **Your homepage displays** section and then choose your newly created page from the **Homepage** drop-down box.

Click the **Save Changes** button to finish.

If you now visit the homepage of your site, you'll no longer see your most recent posts in the main area of the homepage. Instead, you will find the WordPress page you just created.

Depending on the theme you are using, there may not be a header at the top. For example, with the Twenty Twenty-One theme active, I see this:

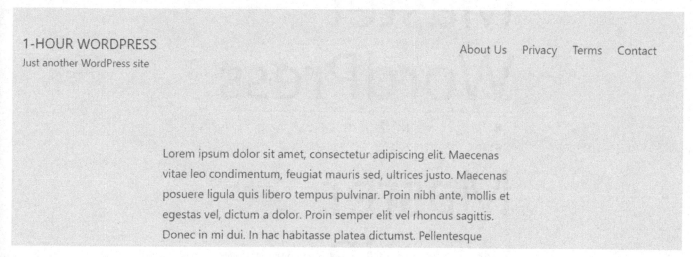

My Master WordPress title is missing. This is a feature of the Twenty Twenty-One theme, removing the title from the page if it is used as a homepage. The Twenty Twenty theme didn't do this:

Master WordPress

Lorem ipsum dolor sit amet, consectetur adipiscing elit. Maecenas vitae
leo condimentum, feugiat mauris sed, ultrices justo. Maecenas posuere
ligula quis libero tempus pulvinar. Proin nibh ante, mollis et egestas vel,
dictum a dolor. Proin semper elit vel rhoncus sagittis. Donec in mi dui.

Of course, I could manually add a heading block and set it to an H1 if I wanted to include a
header on this page:

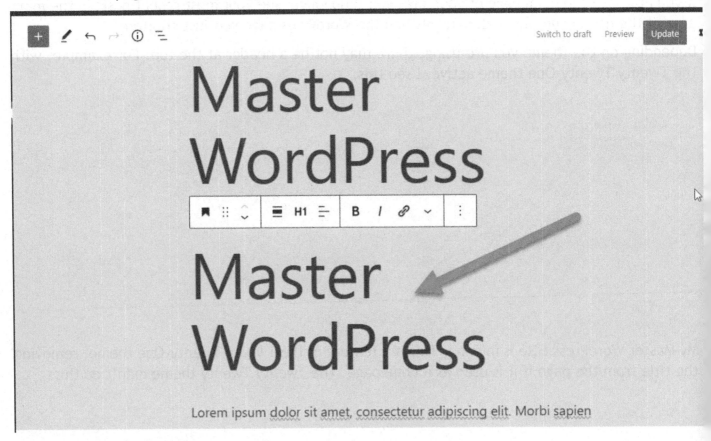

Which results in the following:

You might not like the overall look and feel of your site at the moment. Later in the book, I'll show you how to add a new theme any time you like. It only takes seconds and can completely change the design of your site. You can choose from an almost unlimited variety of styles.

For now, you should concentrate on adding content to the site. For each category you added, you should add some posts.

While you are working on that, we can consider some other important factors, starting with visitor interaction.

Allowing Comments

I love getting comments from real people wanting to engage me on the site or add their own tips, ideas, or thoughts on a post. However, comments are also a major source of frustration because spammers can flood your inbox with hundreds of automated spam comments. Because of this, a lot of webmasters turn them off. You should not turn them off because real visitors like to comment on your posts. Just as importantly, search engines love to see a website that actively engages its visitors.

So, what is the problem with spammers, and how can we stop them?

Well, if you don't already know, you soon will. Spammers see comments on other people's websites as a way to make their own web pages rank better. You see, when a comment is approved, it links back to the website that was entered into the comment form.

So, approved comments are seen as links, and links that point to a site help boost it in Google!

Because of the problems with spammers, we have already set up WordPress so that all comments need to be manually approved. There are also plugins you can install to help cut down on spam comments.

Akismet Anti-Spam

WordPress might install Akismet by default. It is an excellent anti-spam plugin that is free for non-commercial sites. However, if you have a commercial site, the plugin does require you to pay for a commercial license.

When you activate the plugin, you'll get an **Akismet Anti-Spam** item in the **Settings** menu. Click on that to be taken to the setup procedure:

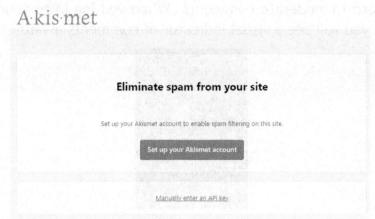

Click the **Set up your Akismet account** button.

You'll be taken to the Akismet website, where you can set up your account. Just follow the instructions on the site to get your API key and connect it to your site.

Moderating Comments

We had already seen the comments screen when we looked at the demo comment installed by WordPress, so you should already have a pretty good idea of how this all works.

When someone comes to your site and leaves a comment, it is checked against our blacklist (we set that up earlier). If the comment contains a word or phrase in the blacklist, it is sent to the spam folder. If it passes the checks, the comment is added to the "Pending" list. At this point, WordPress sends an email to your admin email address telling you there is a comment to moderate. That email is useful because it contains links to approve, trash, or spam the comment.

```
A new comment on the post "WordPress For Beginners 2019 Updates" is waiting for your
approval
https://ezseonews.com/wp4b/

Author:
2601:603:7f:b650:31e0:11c8:55c2:a6e3)
Email:
URL: h
Comment:
Hi Andy,
```

```
Approve it: https://ezseonews.com/wp-admin/comment.php?action=approve&c=18166#wpbody-content
Trash it: https://ezseonews.com/wp-admin/comment.php?action=trash&c=18166#wpbody-content
Spam it: https://ezseonews.com/wp-admin/comment.php?action=spam&c=18166#wpbody-content
Currently 2 comments are waiting for approval. Please visit the moderation panel:
https://ezseonews.com/wp-admin/edit-comments.php?comment_status=moderated#wpbody-content
```

You can click the relevant link in the email to moderate the comment if you like. I personally like to log into the Dashboard to moderate comments. When you log in to your Dashboard and there are comments waiting, you will see a visual indicator of comments awaiting moderation:

Clicking on the **Comments** menu item takes you to the moderation screen.

From there, you can approve the comment or send it to spam or trash.

I highly recommend that you are very strict about approving comments. If you do not know the commenter (i.e., they are not a friend or a frequent visitor you know of), then never approve a comment that does not add to the conversation on the post they are commenting on.

For example, on my web hosting post, I would trash all of the following comments:

> *"Love the site, great work!"*

> *"What theme are you using? It looks great."*

> *"I love this site."*

"Fantastic article. I will send my friend over to read it."

> *"I think you have a problem with browser compatibility."*

Incidentally, these are all very common spam comments whose sole purpose is to get a link back to a website. Quite often, spam comments try to flatter you into approving them.

This type of comment can be easily spotted as they don't usually include any reference to the subject of the post they were left on. These comments could have been made on ANY post. That is often the sign of a spammer at work.

I tend to only approve comments that add to the "discussion" started by the post. I'd also approve a comment that was obviously written by someone who had read the post and wanted help or advice related to the post. Comments are there for you to interact, help, and discuss with your audience. Any comment that does not add to the conversation should be trashed.

When you have comments in the trash or spam folders, you will eventually need to go in and empty the trash (or empty the spam folder). Just click on the tab (in the screenshot below, I have clicked on the **Trash** tab):

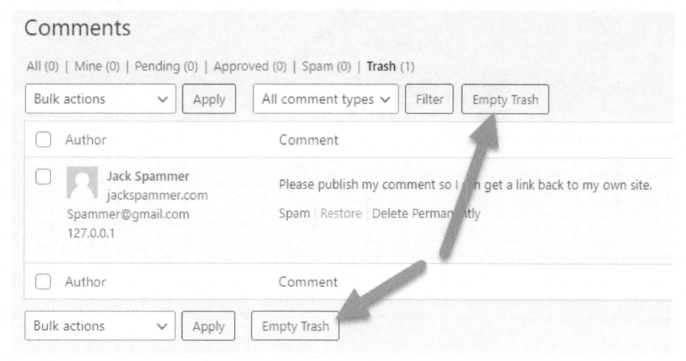

Then click on one of the **Empty Trash** buttons.

On the spam screen, there is an "Empty Spam" button.

So, what is the difference between spam and trash?

Well, there isn't a lot of difference. WordPress and many anti-spam plugins will send suspicious comments to the spam folder as a place to hold them until you moderate them. Everything in the spam folder will be suspicious, so have a quick glance down to see if there is anything worth approving. Some anti-spam plugins will check the IP and email addresses of comments in the spam folder and send any further comments from those "spammers" directly to the spam folder.

If there is anything worth approving, you can move your mouse over the comment and click the "Not Spam" link.

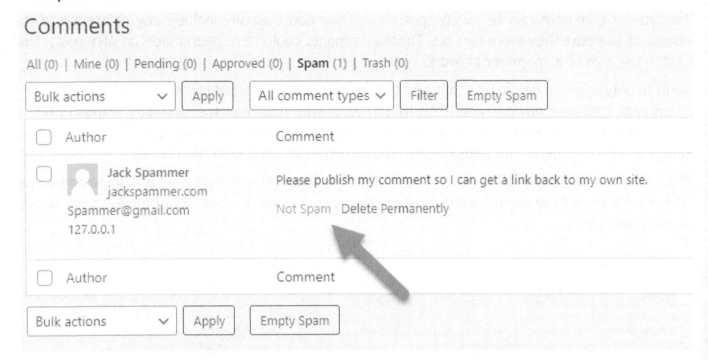

That will send it to the Pending tab.

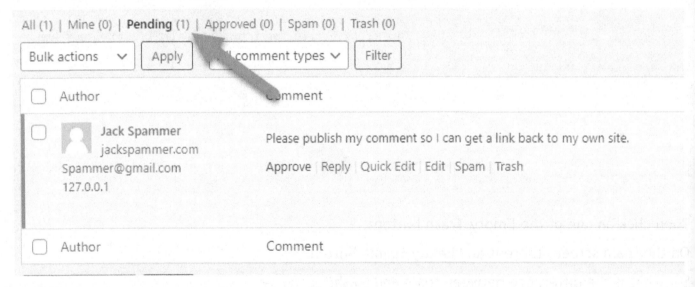

From there, you can approve the comment if you want.

Social Sharing?

Having great content on your site is one thing, but getting people to see it is something else.

One of the ways people find a website is through search engines. If we rank well enough for a particular search term, the web searcher may land on our page.

Another way people can find our content is via social media channels. Places like Facebook and Twitter are good examples. To make this more likely, we need to install a social sharing plugin on the site. A social sharing plugin will add buttons to the website that allow people to share the content they are reading with their followers. Social sharing buttons make sharing easy and, therefore, more likely.

There are several good social sharing plugins, and I do recommend you look around to find one that matches the design of your website. However, to get you started, let's install my current favorite.

Go to **Add New** in the **Plugins** menu. Search for **Grow Social** by Mediavine and look for this one:

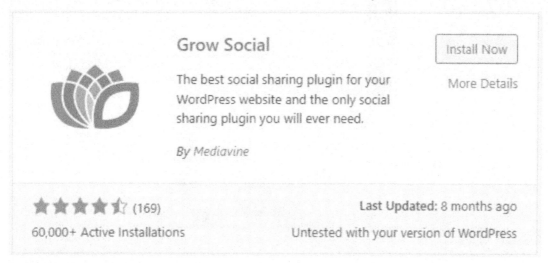

Install and activate the plugin.

You'll see a new menu in the left sidebar labeled **Grow**. Click it.

This plugin offers you two options for displaying social sharing buttons – a floating panel or embedded in your content.

Floating Sidebar   Inline Content

You can use one system or both. To activate a system, click the slider at the bottom. When you do that, a **Settings** button appears:

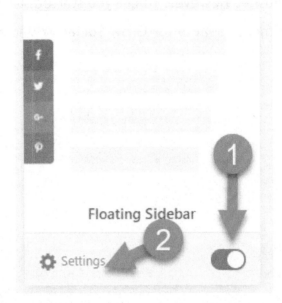

The floating sidebar will create a panel on your web page, which "floats" down the side of your content and is always visible. The inline content option will insert the buttons before and/or after the article on your web page.

Before the social sharing buttons appear on your site, you need to tell the plugin which social accounts you want to include. Click on the settings button.

You can now click the **Select Networks** button to choose which networks you want to work with.

Click on the **Select Networks** button to access the choices.

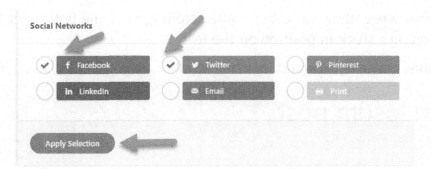

Click the **Apply Selection** button.

The networks will now appear on the settings screen, and you can re-order these by dragging them up or down using the "handle" on the left. You can also delete a network by clicking the "X Remove" link on the right or change the button's label.

Below you'll see some display settings. I'll leave you to explore these options.

When you are ready, scroll to the bottom and make sure that **Post** is checked under the **Post type display settings**. If you want to include sharing buttons on pages, make sure that is checked too.

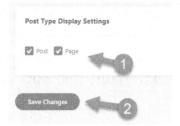

Click **Save Changes**.

If you are using both inline and floating buttons, you need to set them both up separately. You can go back to the main plugin settings by clicking the **Toolkit** link in the sidebar menu.

If you visit your site, you should now see the social sharing buttons on posts (and pages if you enabled that). If you chose a floating sidebar, it looks like this:

Notice that the above screenshot was taken while scrolling near the bottom of the post. The social sharing buttons are stuck in position on the left.

If you chose the inline content, it would look like this:

Obviously, yours won't look exactly like mine, as it depends on the settings you choose. One thing I remove is that **Sharing is caring!** text. You'll find out how to do that in the **Inline Content** settings.

Other Social Share Plugins

Over the years, I have tried lots of social sharing plugins. Some work great, while others only seem to work on some websites and not others. If you find Grow Social does not work properly on *your* site, just search for "social share" in the **Add Plugins** screen and try some.

Website Navigation

Someone landing on your website for the first time will have no idea what content is on your site or how to find it. It is, therefore, vital that you have good website navigation.

On sites I build, I make sure the following navigation is in place:

1. A homepage that tries to help the visitor find what they want. That can literally mean writing out instructions, using graphics, or just making the sidebar and menu navigation speak for themselves.

2. A search box. This can easily be added as a widget. The default search box that comes with WordPress is poor. A better option is to add a custom Google search box that offers far more relevant search results from your site. It is beyond the scope of this book to show you how to do this, but Google it if interested.

3. A main menu offering contact, about, and other "legal" pages. This does not always need to be in the header area of your site. I often put this type of menu in the footer widget area.

4. A recent posts widget so visitors can quickly see the recent articles I have written. We saw the recent posts plugin earlier in the book.

5. Every post on my site will have a related posts section, which lists other posts that I think a visitor may be interested in.

The only one on that list we have not seen so far is the related posts plugin. Let's install and configure that now.

Related Posts

The plugin I recommend you use for related posts is called **Yet Another Related Posts** (YARPP to its friends). This plugin allows you to set up a "Related Articles" section at the end of your posts. This will automatically create links to related articles on your site.

Go to the **Add New** Plugin screen and search for **yarpp**.

Install and activate the plugin.

You will now find the **YARPP** menu inside the main **Settings** menu. Click on **YARPP** so we can set this up.

At the top of the YARPP settings is "The Pool." The pool is the set of posts that can be used for building a related articles section. If you decide you don't want any posts from a particular category showing up in related article sections, you can exclude that category here by checking the box next to that category. You can do the same with Tags if you have defined any.

There is also an option to limit the age of posts in the pool, only including posts from the previous X days, weeks, or months.

I am going to leave the pool defaults as they are.

If you think you won't be changing these settings, you can hide "The Pool" by unchecking the option in the **Screen Options** (at the top of your screen).

The next settings on the page are **The Algorithm**. This defines how closely related an article needs to be, to be shown as a "related post."

I recommend you leave the relatedness options with their default values for now. You can play with the **Match Threshold** option, increasing it a little when you have some posts on your site to make sure you are getting suggestions that are related to each post.

Next up are the **Automatic Display Options**.

There is plenty of scope for playing around here as well, including using your own template, but we are going to use the default settings, with one exception. Place a checkmark next to **Show excerpt?** This will give our related posts a description. When you check that box, a few more options appear. Change **Excerpt length** to 50 (I recommend that you experiment with this setting).

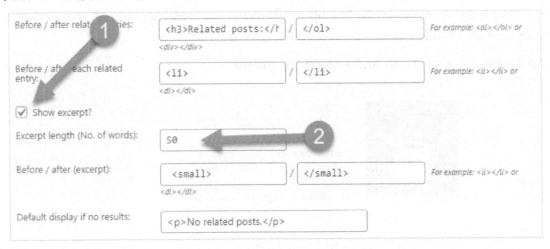

Ok, that is all we are changing. Scroll to the bottom and click **Save Changes**.

You will now have a related posts section at the end of every post on the site. You probably won't see much yet because you don't have content on the site. Here is what I see at the end of my post on this demo site:

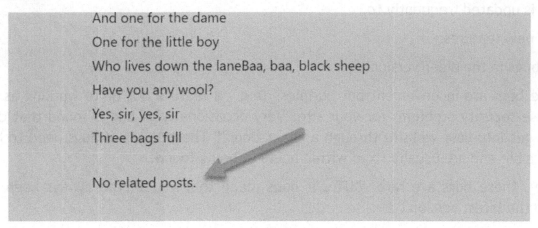

And one for the dame

One for the little boy

Who lives down the laneBaa, baa, black sheep

Have you any wool?

Yes, sir, yes, sir

Three bags full

No related posts.

However, as you start adding content, the related posts section will start to populate with recommendations for your visitors. If it doesn't, then play around with the **Match Threshold** in **The Algorithm** settings. Reducing it should result in more matches.

Here is an example of a related posts section on one of my sites using this plugin.

Related Posts

1. What Is an Attachment in WordPress?

   WordPress posts and pages can contain attachments. They include images, videos, podcasts, and various documents, etc. Used correctly, attachments enhance the visitor experience and improve SE rankings.

2. What Is A Shortcode in WordPress?

   Learn about WordPress shortcode and how it puts the power of coding into the hands of every site owner. No Skills Needed! It's a fast, immediate, and cool way to add dynamic website features.

3. What Is a WordPress Favicon and How to Create One?

   Read this quick quite on the 3 ways to create and install a custom favicon in WordPress. Websites with favicons look more professional, enhance the site's reputation, and have higher trust levels.

This "related posts" section was on an article about WordPress on my ezSEONews.com site. Can you see the benefits? People who are reading the main WordPress article are shown other articles that are related to what they've just been reading about. It gives us another chance to keep the visitor on our site.

Keeping WordPress Updated & Secure

WordPress is updated frequently to:

1. Add new features.

2. Fix bugs in the older version.

While some bugs are inconvenient but harmless (e.g., a feature not quite working as it should), others cause security problems for your site. Very occasionally, a bug is found that could allow hackers to get into your website through a "back door." These types of bugs need to be fixed as soon as possible and are usually fixed within hours of being found.

Fortunately, these bugs are rare. BUT... it does mean that you should always keep WordPress updated to the latest version.

When you installed your site, you may have had the option to enable an auto-upgrade script, so upgrades will be largely automatic.

If you don't have automatic updates "switched on," don't worry. Upgrading manually is very easy.

When you log in to the Dashboard, there is an **Updates** item in the **Dashboard** menu.

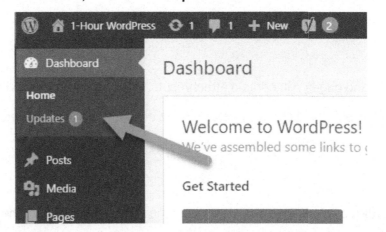

This will notify us when there are updates available, much like the notification we saw earlier with comments to moderate. You can then click through to the **Updates** area and update the files.

The "Updates" area lists all available updates for WordPress itself, plugins, and themes.

When a WordPress upgrade is available, you'll see something like this in your main Dashboard:

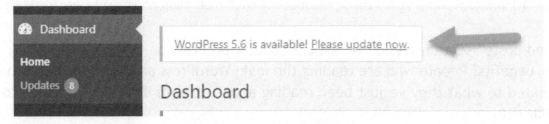

That **Please update now** link will take you to the **Dashboard, Updates** page, which looks like this:

An updated version of WordPress is available.

You can update to WordPress 5.6 automatically:

Update Now

While your site is being updated, it will be in maintenance mode. As soon as your updates are complete, this mode will be deactivated.

Just click the **Update Now** button, and the upgrade will proceed automatically on its own. You may have to click a button or two to "upgrade the database" or some other task, but that's as technical as it gets. Just follow the instructions on the screen, and you'll be fine.

If there are plugins to update, you'll see something like this:

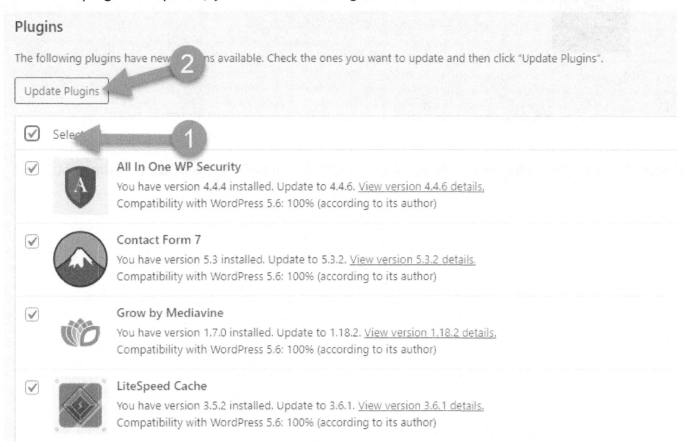

Plugins

The following plugins have new ~~ns available. Check the ones you want to update and then click "Update Plugins".

Update Plugins

☑ Selec~

☑ **All In One WP Security**
You have version 4.4.4 installed. Update to 4.4.6. View version 4.4.6 details.
Compatibility with WordPress 5.6: 100% (according to its author)

☑ **Contact Form 7**
You have version 5.3 installed. Update to 5.3.2. View version 5.3.2 details.
Compatibility with WordPress 5.6: 100% (according to its author)

☑ **Grow by Mediavine**
You have version 1.7.0 installed. Update to 1.18.2. View version 1.18.2 details.
Compatibility with WordPress 5.6: 100% (according to its author)

☑ **LiteSpeed Cache**
You have version 3.5.2 installed. Update to 3.6.1. View version 3.6.1 details.
Compatibility with WordPress 5.6: 100% (according to its author)

You can check one or more plugins to update, or click the **Select All** checkbox, which selects all plugins for updating. Then, simply click the **Update Plugins** button, and WordPress does the rest for you.

When your theme(s) needs updating, you'll see something like this on the updates page:

Themes

The following themes have new versions available. Check the ones you want to update and then click "Update Themes".

Please Note: Any customizations you have made to theme files will be lost. Please consider using child themes for modifications

Update Themes

☐ Se

☐ **Twenty Twenty-One**
You have version 1.0 installed. Update to 1.1.

☐ **Customizr Pro**
You have version 2.3.6 installed. Update to 2.4.3.

☐ Select All

Update Themes

Check the box next to the theme(s) you want to update, and click the **Update Themes** button.

Backing up the Site

Backing up anything on a computer should be a priority. While good web hosts do keep backups for you, if your site gets infected with any kind of malicious code and you don't find out about it for a while, all of your backups can be infected and, therefore, not much use.

I always recommend you have some kind of backup plan, and fortunately, there is a great plugin that can help.

UpdraftPlus

Backing up anything on a computer should be a priority. While good web hosts do keep backups for you, if your site gets infected with any kind of malicious code and you don't find out about it for a while, all their backups could be infected.

I always recommend you have your own backup plan, and fortunately, there is a great plugin that can help.

Click the **Add New** item in the **Plugins** menu.

Search for **Updraft**.

Find and install this plugin:

After clicking the **Install Now** button, the installation process will proceed. Once complete, this button changes to say **Activate**. Click to activate the plugin.

You'll have a new **UpdraftPlus Backups** section in the settings menu.

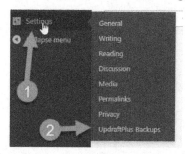

169

Click on it to access the settings of this plugin.

You can take manual backups on the **Backup/Restore** tab:

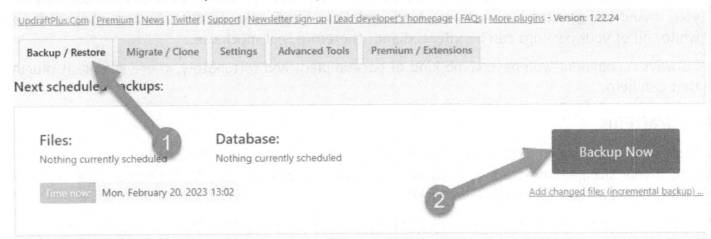

More powerful still is the ability to schedule automatic backups of your site. To do that, click on the **Settings** tab.

Choose a frequency and the number of backups to retain.

Now scroll down and click **Save Changes** at the bottom.

You will notice that on this screen, you also have the option of using remote storage for your backups. If you have a Dropbox account, that is a great place to send backups. They'll be off your server and safe if you ever need them. You can also get backups emailed to you, though full backups can be very large.

I won't go into details on setting this up. Just follow the instructions that are included with the plugin.

Changing the Look & Feel of the site

By now, you should have a fully functioning website and know how to add more content to the site. However, you might not like the look of your site. Maybe the colors, the fonts, or the layout doesn't look right to you. That is where themes come in.

WordPress was created to be modular in nature so that developers could create add-ons. We've seen some of these in the form of plugins and widgets, but another major way you can customize your site is by changing the WordPress theme.

Think of themes as skins. You can add a skin over the top of your content, which changes the look and feel but doesn't touch your underlying data (content, installed plugins, etc.).

The quickest way to experience themes is to look at the ones WordPress installed on your server when you installed WordPress.

Go to **Themes** in the **Appearance** menu of your Dashboard.

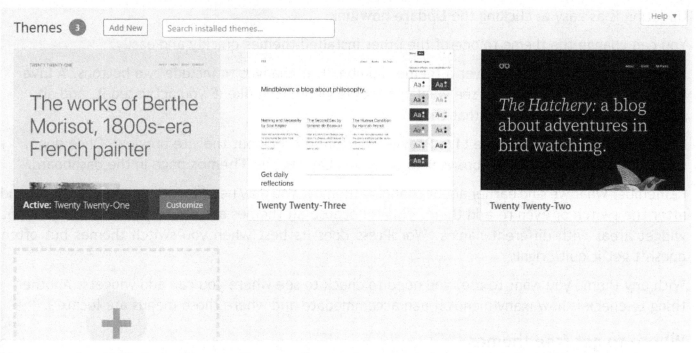

Here you should find the Twenty Twenty-One and some of the other default WordPress themes. Incidentally, this view will also show you if there are any updates available for installed themes. My Twenty Twenty-One theme has a pending update:

171

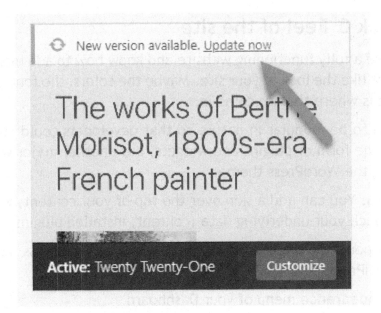

Updating is as easy as clicking the **Update now** link.

You can change the theme to one of the other installed themes quickly and easily.

When you move your mouse over a theme thumbnail, it changes to include two buttons. A **Live Preview** button allows you to see what the theme would look like IF you activated it, and an **Activate** button to change to that theme.

For a quick check, click on the **Live Preview** button to check out the site preview. Once done, click the back button of your browser to bring you back to the **Themes** page in the dashboard.

Remember what we said earlier about changing themes? You may need to move your widgets around after the switch or even re-add them. This is because all themes are different and have different widget areas with different names. WordPress does its best when you switch themes but often doesn't get it quite right.

With any theme you want to use, you need to check to see where you can add widgets. Another thing to check is how many menus it can accommodate and where those menus are located.

Where to get free themes

WordPress makes it easy for you to find and install themes for your site.

Click on **Themes** in the **Appearance** menu.

At the top of the Theme page, click the **Add New** button.

You will be taken to an "Add Themes" screen.

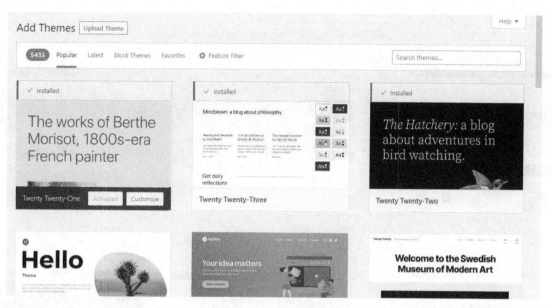

At the very top of this screen is an **Upload Theme** button. If you've bought or downloaded a theme from a website, it will be zipped up. Just click the Upload Theme button and upload the zipped file. The theme will install, and you can then preview or activate it.

Next, on this screen, you'll see a menu across the top, with "Popular" selected. This menu gives you access to "Popular," "Latest," and "Block Themes" in the WordPress repository. Click the menu item that interests you and browse the themes.

The final option in the menu is the "Feature Filter." This is where you can filter out the free themes according to the features you want.

For example, if I wanted to search for a three-column theme that allows a custom header and is suitable for an education niche site, then I'd search for:

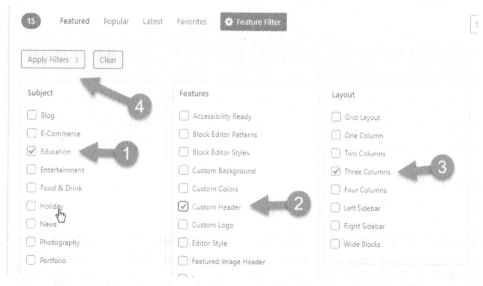

On clicking the **Apply Filters** button, any matches are displayed and appear in the search results:

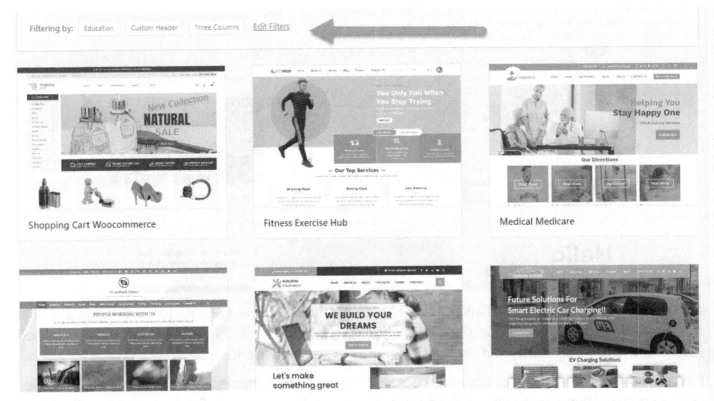

Shopping Cart Woocommerce   Fitness Exercise Hub   Medical Medicare

EV Charging Solutions

Mouse over each theme in turn to show details for the theme. From this preview, you can:

1. Click **Details & Preview** (or just the Preview button) to get more information about the theme, including a preview.

2. Click the **Install button** to install the theme into your Dashboard.

Note that when you install a new theme, your old one remains in the dashboard. This makes it easy to switch between themes you've installed.

The biggest problem with a lot of free themes is that they have a link back to the creator's website in the footer. This is bad from a search engine point of view, and I do not recommend you use any theme that forces this link on your site.

The WordPress themes we saw earlier do contain links to WordPress, but that is a little different. WordPress is a huge authority site, the creators of the theme and creators of your content management system (CMS). Besides, you can remove that link if you want to.

Customizing a theme

This section refers to non-FSE-enabled themes only.

WordPress has a simple point-and-click interface to help you customize your active theme. However, the customizations that are available to you are dictated by the theme itself. Some themes have very few customizations, while others will offer you pages and pages of custom settings.

There are a couple of ways you can get to the Customize screen. The first is by clicking the **Customize** button on the thumbnail of the active theme in the Themes screen (Appearance -> Themes):

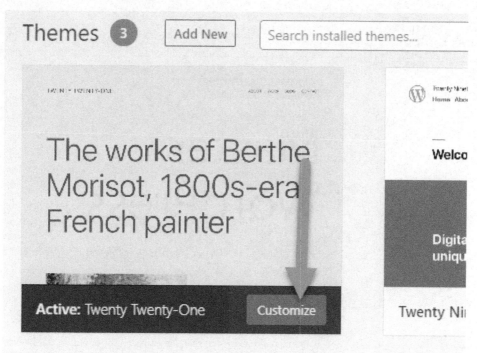

The second method is by clicking **Customize** in the **Appearance** menu:

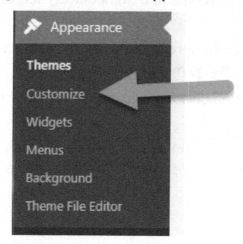

Both of these options will open up the "customize" screen:

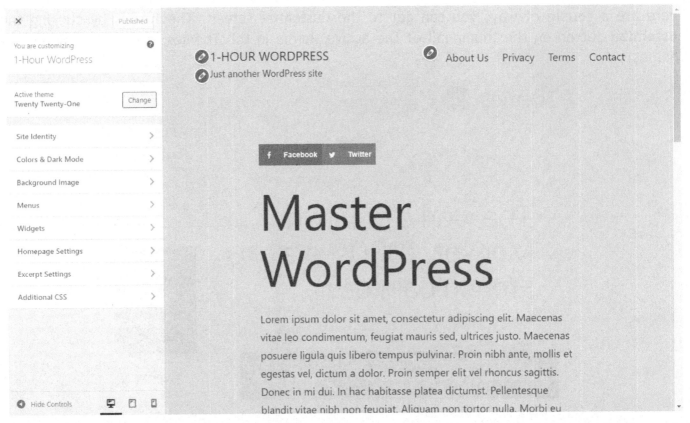

The customization options are on the left of the screen, and a live preview of your site is on the right. This allows you to tweak your theme and immediately see the effects of those tweaks in the live preview.

Many of the customizations available here are also accessible via the standard sidebar menus in WordPress (mainly through the **Settings** menu).

Remember that these customization options are specific to the theme you are using. You may see different options for your theme.

The options are grouped into related items. To open these groups, click on the little arrow to the right of the group name. You can explore these options for yourself, but I will mention one item on this **Customize** screen.

Additional CSS

Although CSS is beyond the scope of this book, if you know how to use CSS, you can add custom CSS to style your web pages.

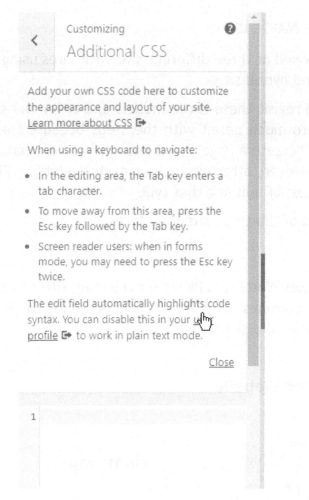

The CSS you add to this box will override the CSS that is built into your theme. Therefore you can override much of the formatting forced upon you by the theme to something you choose.

Go through the rest of the options on the customize screen. You won't break anything in this area of WordPress, so have fun and explore.

Building the 3 Site Models

Earlier in the book, we looked at three different site structures using posts and pages. These were the business site, blog, and hybrid site.

In this chapter, I want to revisit these three models and cover the steps required to create each one. I won't be going into much detail with the steps because the "how-to" has already been covered. e.g., I may say, "create a Page." You know how to do that, so there is no need for more instruction than that. However, after we look at each model, I will give you a link to a video I created showing the process of building that type of site.

I'll start by reminding you of the three site structures.

A Business Site

A business site typically uses WordPress Pages for the main site content rather than posts. However, it is common for business sites also to include a blog where the business can make announcements. Here is that site structure:

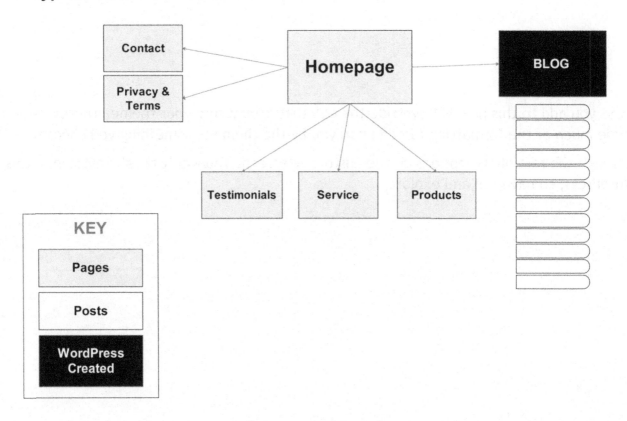

A Typical Business Website

Before we look at the steps to create this type of site structure, I need to introduce you to a new concept that works nicely on Business style sites when you need to set up a blog.

The Posts Page

One feature you may find useful in WordPress is the ability to create a "Posts Page." The posts page does what its name suggests - it displays all of the WordPress posts on this page.

This feature is most useful for a business-type site, where most of the site is built with Pages, but you want to have a blog, e.g., for company announcements.

Creating a Posts Page

1. Create a new blank page and publish it. I'll call mine "Blog."

2. Go to the reading settings, and set the **Posts page** to the blank page you just created:

3. Save the settings.

Visit the page, and you'll see that all posts on the site are now listed on this "posts page."

OK, we have enough to continue.

Steps to Create this Business Site

1. Create the Contact, Terms, and Privacy pages.

2. Create the Homepage.

3. Create the following business pages: Testimonials, Services & Products.

4. Create a blank Blog page.

5. Assign the Blog page you created to the Posts Page in the Reading Settings.

6. Write some blog posts.

7. Create a Legal Menu with contact, privacy & Terms, and insert it into the footer of your site.

8. Create a Top Menu with Testimonials, Services, Products & Blog pages included. Insert the menu into the header of the site.

To watch a typical business structure being built, watch this video:

https://ezseonews.com/wp4b-tutorials/#business

A Blog

A typical blog is based on WordPress posts to create an organized, chronological sequence of web pages. The homepage of a blog is typically just a list of all the posts in chronological order. However, you can also create a blog-style site that has a static homepage. WordPress pages will only be used for contact, privacy, etc. Here is that structure:

A Typical Blog

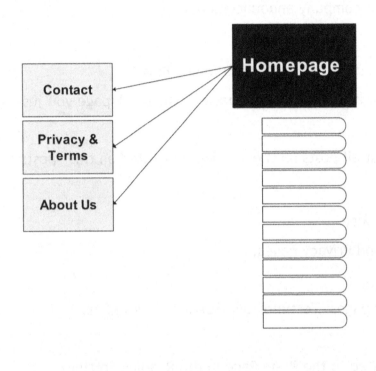

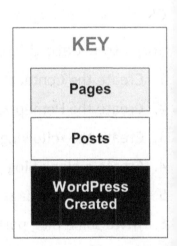

Steps to Create this Blog Site

1. Create Contact, Privacy, Terms, and About Us as WordPress pages.

2. Create a Legal menu, including links to Contact, Privacy, Terms, and About Us.

3. Add the menu to the top of your website.

4. Write some blog posts. These will appear on your homepage.

5. Alternatively, you can create a static homepage and a Blog page. You would then need a menu to direct visitors to the blog.

To watch a typical blog structure being built, watch this video:

https://ezseonews.com/wp4b-tutorials/#blog

A Niche Website (Typical Site)

The typical WordPress website (I often call a Hybrid site) has a static homepage and a number of posts organized into categories. There will be a few WordPress pages for contact, privacy, etc. The site may or may not have a separate blog. Here is that structure:

A Typical Niche Site

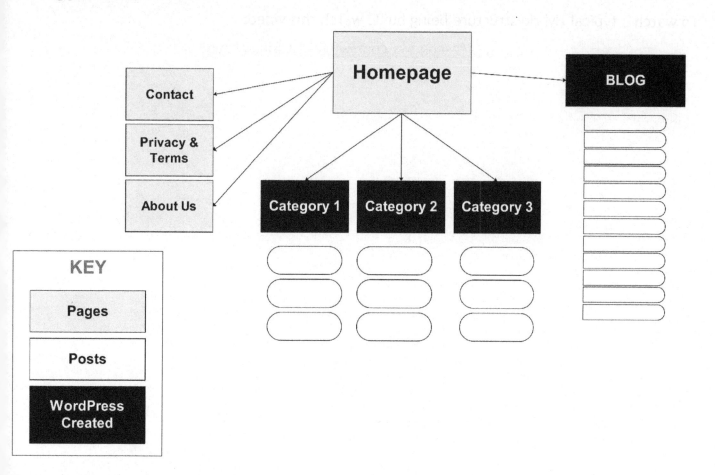

Steps to Create this Niche Site

1. Create Contact, Privacy, Terms & About Us as pages.

2. Create a page to be used as your homepage.

3. In Reading Settings, change the settings to show your static homepage on the homepage of your site.

4. Create categories for all content you want to include on your site, and start writing posts in each of those categories.

5. Create a special **Blog** category that you can use for a separate blog.

6. Start writing some blog posts.

7. Create a legal menu including Contact, Privacy, and Terms, and place this menu in your site's footer.

8. Create a menu containing your categories and put that menu in the most appropriate place. If your site has a sidebar, that would be a good place. You also need to have a link to your blog somewhere, so put that in the same menu, or perhaps a **Top Menu** that also includes a link **Home**.

To watch a typical Hybrid structure being built, watch this video:

https://ezseonews.com/wp4b-tutorials/#hybrid

Beginner's Mistakes

There are several simple mistakes that beginners make when they build a site with WordPress. This chapter lists some of those mistakes.

Post & Page Titles

No two posts should have the same title on your site. No two pages should have the same title, either. A post should not use the same title as a page and vice versa. All posts and pages must have unique titles.

If you use the same title on two documents, Google will think you have two articles on the same topic and wonder why. When Google starts getting confused about the content on your site, you are at the beginning of a very slippery slope.

In addition, if you give two posts the same title, the filename automatically generated by WordPress will mean both filenames are nearly the same. WordPress handles duplicate filenames by adding numbers to the end. If you created three pages with the title "contact," WordPress would give them these filenames:

1. Contact
2. Contact-1
3. Contact-2

Tags & Category Names

Never use the same word or phrase for a category name AND a tag. A phrase can be EITHER a category OR a tag, but not both.

Similarly, never use a word or phrase that you have used as a page/post title as either a tag or category.

For example, suppose you had a health site.

If you had a category called diabetes, you could not use the word diabetes as a post/page title or a tag. You could have a page/post title or tag that included the word diabetes as a longer phrase, like "gestational diabetes" or "pre-diabetes."

Using Tags

Never use more than 4 or 5 tags on a post. Tags should be there to help visitors, so giving visitors long lists of tags will make them useless. Also, indiscriminate use of tags means you'll end up with a lot of tag pages, each listing very few posts. Remember what I said earlier in the book. No tag should be used if it is only being used on one post (or two, and maybe even three depending on the size of your site).

Search Engine Visibility

There is a setting in WordPress that will basically make your site invisible to search engines.

Go to **Reading** in the **Settings** menu.

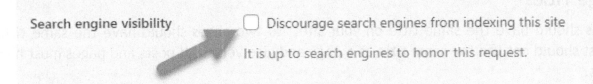

Search engine visibility ☐ Discourage search engines from indexing this site

It is up to search engines to honor this request.

This checkbox is there to stop search engines from finding, spidering, and including your site in the search results. Some webmasters use this when they are initially building a site and then uncheck it when they want to open the site to the public. However, this is not necessary. I'd recommend you leave this unchecked at all times.

If you do find that your site isn't getting indexed and included in Google, do check this setting.

Spam Comments

Over the years, I have seen a number of my students commit this sin. They'll approve a comment on their site simply because the comment is flattering to them. We've talked about this type of comment before. My advice to you is simple. No matter how few comments you may have, NEVER approve a comment that does not add to the conversation of the post it will appear on.

NEVER!

No really. I mean it.

NEVER!

Plugins for all occasions

We have already installed and used some great WordPress plugins. However, there are thousands more out there. In this chapter, I'll list a few more plugins that I have found to be the most useful on my own sites. Some of these plugins are used on all of my WordPress sites, while others are only used for more specific projects.

To keep this book shorter, I will list the most important plugins I regularly use, with a description of what they do.

All-In-One Security & Firewall

As the name suggests, this is an all-in-one security plugin for your site. It is quite complex, so I don't recommend you just install it and enable all the features. I created a tutorial video for enabling "safe" measures here:

https://ezseonews.com/security

Pretty Link Lite

Pretty Link Lite is a free plugin that allows you to create "prettier" links from longer, "uglier" links. It also allows you to track links.

Why might you want to do this?

We'll mention affiliate programs in the next chapter, and these have notoriously ugly long links. Pretty Link Lite is a great way to make those links more manageable.

Find it in the plugin repository.

Dynamic Widgets

Dynamic Widgets is a free plugin that allows you to choose specific pages, posts, categories, etc., to display widgets on. I use this on most of my sites so that I can create custom sidebars for different categories on the site. If someone is reading a post on my site about web hosting, I can make sure that they see web hosting-related advertising in the sidebar.

I also usually create a unique sidebar for my homepage.

I believe that Google prefers websites that don't have the exact same sidebars & footers on all web pages. This plugin helps you achieve that since you can control which widgets appear on which pages and in which widgetized areas of the page.

Find it in the plugin repository.

W3 Total Cache

W3 Total Cache is a free plugin to speed up your site. It is a little complicated to set up but well worth the effort.

Find it in the plugin repository.

Wishlist Member

Wishlist Member is a commercial plugin that allows you to set up a membership site (paid or free) on your website. I have used it in the past to set up membership sites. It integrates nicely with WordPress and will integrate payment gateways like Paypal.

https://ezseonews.com/wlm

wpForo Forum

wpForo Forum is a free plugin that allows you to set up a forum on your site. If you want to grow a community on your website, this plugin can create a forum on your site with a few mouse clicks.

Making Money with your website

There are a lot of different ways you can make money with your website. I won't go into too much detail in this book, but I will briefly discuss the options.

All the following forms of site monetization are free to join and do not cost anything to run on your website.

Affiliate programs

An affiliate program (sometimes called a partner program) is a good way to make some money from your site. A lot of great companies run them, and you can apply to join relevant programs.

Amazon has a great affiliate program. When you join, you can link to any product on the Amazon website from your own website using a link that Amazon gives you. This link is long and ugly, which is where Pretty Link Lite comes in. If someone goes through your link and buys something, you get a commission.

The amount of commission you get with affiliate programs varies enormously. For example, Amazon pays around 4% - 8% of the order value, but they convert customers very well.

Other sites like Clickbank specialize in digital products (eBooks & software). The average commission is probably around 50%, but you can earn 75% commission on some products, sometimes even more than that.

Shareasale and Commission Junction are two affiliate networks I use. An affiliate network is a company that works with other companies that want to run an affiliate program. You can sign up at Shareasale and/or Commission Junction (often just referred to as CJ), then apply to join affiliate programs on their books. Some affiliate programs will accept you immediately; others require a manual review of your site and application. However, it is typically very easy to join affiliate programs through both of these networks. If you make a commission on a network, the network collects the commissions for you and then pays you every month.

Google Adsense

When you visit Google and search for something, the top few results are typically adverts related to what you searched for. Companies are paying for these adverts.

If you click on one of these adverts on Google, the company that paid for the advert pays Google some money. The amount they have to pay is based on the "cost per click" (or CPC) value of that advert. Adverts in more competitive niches cost more, so the CPC is higher.

Google Adsense is a program that allows you to put similar "Adsense" adverts on your website. When someone clicks on one of these Adsense adverts on your site, Google gets paid the CPC by the company that owns the advert. Google then shares this money with you.

Appendix I - Full Site Editor (FSE Primer)

This book has looked at using WordPress with a non-FSE-enabled theme because Full Site Editing is not a beginner's topic and is currently still in beta. Serious web designers with lots of experience in WordPress will use this eventually, but it's still buggy and lacks a lot of features needed for complete control over site design.

Having said that, FSE is the most exciting thing to come to WordPress since the introduction of plugins, so I wanted to give you a quick primer on what it is and what it can (or will be able to) do.

I suggest you follow along with your own copy of WordPress as we go through this chapter. It is a complete tutorial to get you up and running with the full site editor. By the end of this chapter, you'll have a good basic knowledge of how you can use the FSE to make design changes to every aspect of your site. OK, let's start.

To use FSE, you need to activate an FSE-enabled theme.

If you go to the **Themes** menu inside **Appearance**, we can install one.

Click the **Add new** button and search for **Twenty**. Install and activate the Twenty Twenty-Three theme. This is the latest theme from WordPress and is FSE-enabled.

Once enabled, you'll see the **Appearance** menu has changed. A lot!

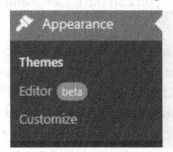

If you don't see **Customize**, don't worry. That is only in my screenshot because I have Yoast SEO installed on the site, and that plugin is adding the Customize link. New installs will only have **Themes** and **Editor (beta)**.

Click on the **Editor** menu.

This opens the Full Site Editor.

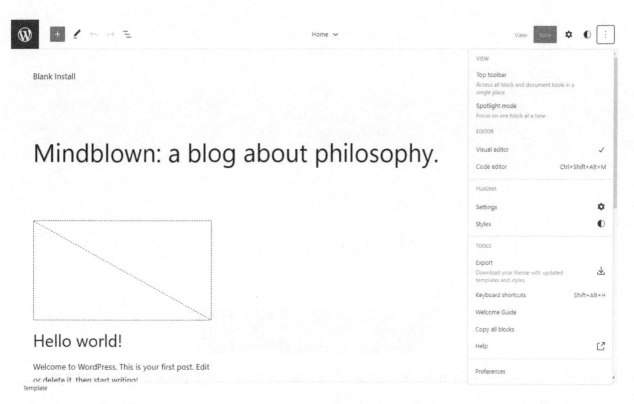

Click the WordPress logo in the top left to see a sidebar:

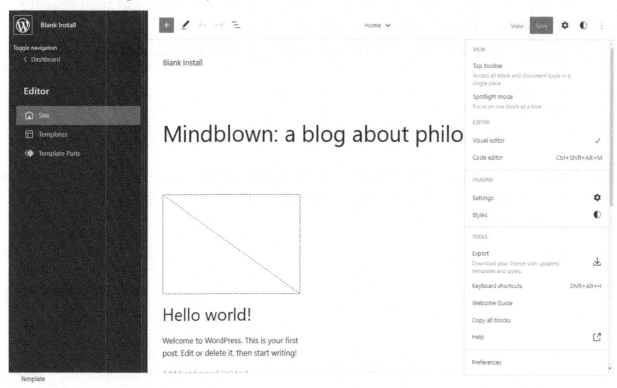

At the top center, you can see "Home." Click the little down arrow next to the "home," and you'll get a drop-down menu:

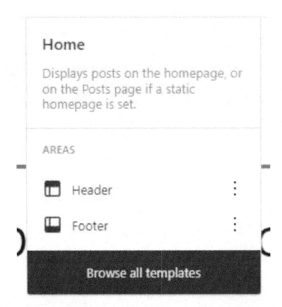

At the top, it tells you that this template displays posts or a static page on the homepage, whichever is configured in the reading settings.

There are two areas marked called **Header** and **Footer**. These are "parts" of the template, something that FSE calls **Template Parts,** which we will explore later.

Click on **Header,** and the header part of the template is selected in the editor.

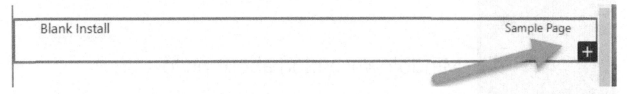

It's basic, but you can see the + on the right to add blocks to the header area. But what are those other items in the header? The "Blank Install" and the "Sample Page" text?

Click to open the **List View.**

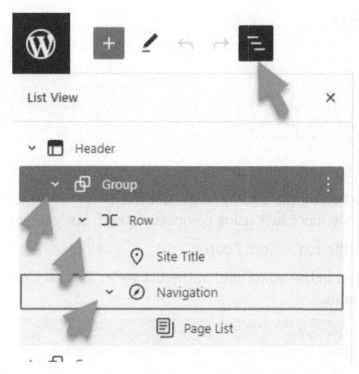

You can see the blocks that make up the **Header**. There is a **Group** block that contains a **Row** block. Expand the row block, and you'll see it contains a **Site Title** block ("Blank Install" in my example) and a **Navigation** block. Expand the navigation block, and you'll see it contains a **Page List** block (which is displaying "Sample Page" in my example).

Selecting any of these blocks in the list view will select them in the editing window, and you'll get a popup menu for the selected block so you can edit properties. If you open the **Settings** pane (the cog), you'll see you have access to the block properties exactly as we saw in the Gutenberg chapter of this book.

Let's add a logo to the header.

With **Site Title** selected in the list view, open the **Options** menu, and select **Insert before**. This will add a blank paragraph block. Click into it and start typing **/site**. Select **Site Logo** from the popup screen. A site logo block will be added.

Click the upload icon to upload a logo, or choose one from your media library. The image will appear in the header section:

Blank Install   Sample Page

You can adjust its width and other properties if you select it.

If you want to adjust the horizontal spacing, e.g., put the Site Title next to the logo, then a row won't work, and you'd have more luck using columns instead, but you get the idea.

From the **Home** menu at the top, select **Footer**.

The footer will be selected in the editor and in the list view. Expand the blocks in the list view to see what the footer contains.

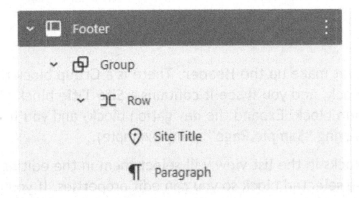

The footer is contained within a **Group** block, so all elements of the footer can be treated as a single entity. Inside the Group is a **Row** block. This will align any blocks within the row horizontally. You can see a **Site Title** block and a **Paragraph** block. What if I want to centrally align the Site title and copyright, stacked on top of each other? Let's do it.

Select the **Paragraph** block and you'll see the "Proudly powered by WordPress" text selected in the editor. Change that to a copyright notice:

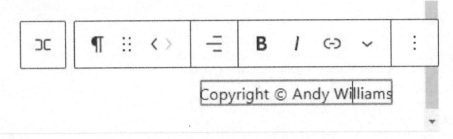

In the **List** View, select the **Site Title** block in the footer. Click the **Options** menu for that block and **Remove Site Title**. The site title will disappear, and the copyright will align to the left in the

row. The row is not really needed now as it is designed to create a row of blocks, and we only have one block. In the **List View**, drag the **Paragraph** block above the **Group** block and drop it. Now delete the **Group** with the **Row.**

Align the paragraph block to the center using the paragraph menu.

Click the **Options** menu for the **Paragraph** block and select **Insert Before.**

A blank paragraph block will be inserted. Click into that and type **/site.** Select **Site Title** from the menu that appears. Align that centrally.

We've just made some changes to the footer area of our site using the Full Site Editor!

Save your changes and visit your site. You should see the site title and copyright at the bottom, central and stacked one on the other:

Blank Install

Copyright © Andy Williams

Go back to the Full Site Editor and look at the **List View** again.

If we collapse everything down, you can see three main entries:

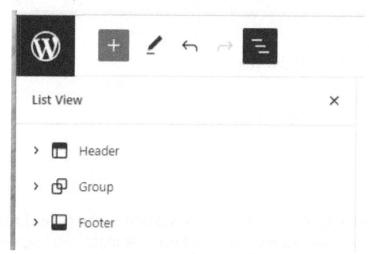

We've seen the header and footer already. You can go in and edit these, as we've just seen. In non-FSE-enabled themes, the header and footer are controlled 100% by the theme you are using, not WordPress. FSE changed all that.

But what about that **Group** block in the middle? Expand it to see what is in the group:

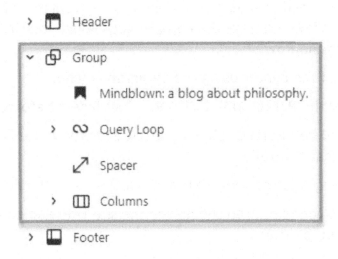

At the top is a **Heading** block that shows the title of the post or page.

Next is a **Query** block. If you select it, you can see what the query block contains in the editor.

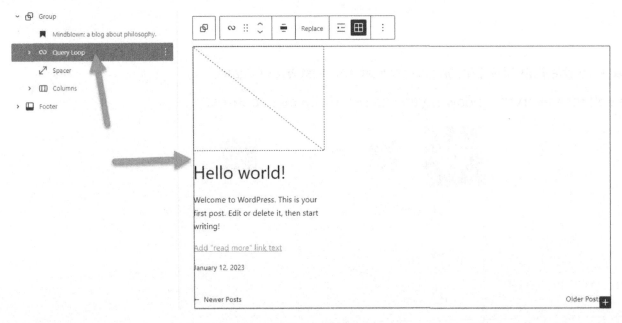

It contains the post or page content that will be rendered to the page. Expand the **Query Loop** block in the list view. The query loop contains a **Post Template** and **Pagination**. Both can be expanded. The pagination has a **Previous Page** and a **Next Page,** which correspond to the "Newer Posts" and "Older Posts" links after the post.

The **Post Template** contains the following blocks:

1. Post Featured Image
2. Post Title
3. Post Excerpt
4. Post Date

5. Spacer (to provide some space between the end of the post and the pagination.

Select the **Spacer** block and increase/decrease the size of the space to get an idea of how this works. See the space in the edit window change as you drag the spacer handle.

OK, what if you don't want your posts to show a featured image?

Simple. Just delete it.

Select it in the list view and use the **Options** menu to remove it. Don't forget to save your work.

The **Query Loop** will go to your WordPress database and pull out the relevant information for the web page you are loading. We aren't going to go into how this works, but if you select the query loop in the list view and open the properties panel on the right (the cog button), you'll see a setting that makes the magic happen.

Settings

 Inherit query from template

Toggle to use the global query context that is set with the current template, such as an archive or search. Disable to customize the settings independently.

What this setting does is makes sure the query loop will get the correct data for the type of web page being viewed. With WordPress themes, it is possible to use the same template for every page on your site. That means the same template can be used to display a post, page, category page, tag page, author page, homepage, etc. Now clearly, these are all a little different and require different data from the database. The **Inherit query from template** will make sure that the correct data is pulled from the database to use with whatever page is being displayed.

However, the beauty of WordPress is that you can create separate templates for every type of web page your site displays. You can create a template for posts, one for pages, one for category pages, one for tag pages, one for author pages, one for a search results page, one to display a 404 message, and so on. This level of control means you can customize every different type of page to your liking.

Pull down the **Home** menu at the top of the screen and select **Browse all Templates**. The sidebar opens with three entries. Site, Templates, and Template parts.

The **Site** is the area we have just been looking at. This is the "homepage" template, but it will also be used as a general "default" template for your site if a more appropriate template cannot be found for a particular type of page. E.g., if you don't create an archive template, this template can be used to display archives too.

Click on **Templates** in the left sidebar. The current templates for the theme are shown on the right.

Template	Added by
Home Displays posts on the homepage, or on the Posts page if a static homepage is set.	Twenty Twenty-Three
404 Displays when no content is found.	Twenty Twenty-Three
Archive Displays post categories, tags, and other archives.	Twenty Twenty-Three
Blank	Twenty Twenty-Three
Blog (Alternative)	Twenty Twenty-Three
Index Displays posts.	Twenty Twenty-Three

There are more than shown in that screenshot, but you get the idea. If a category page is being loaded into a browser, the **Archive** template will be used. If a page cannot be found in a web browser, the **404** template will be used. If a page is being displayed, it will use the **Page** template. If a post is being displayed, the **Post** template will be displayed. And so on.

These templates are included in the Twenty Twenty-Three theme and make up a collection of templates that cover every type of webpage your site will use. But it is not an exhaustive list. For example, the **Archive** template will be used for all archives, like category pages, tag pages, etc. But what if you want to use one template for tag pages and a different template for category pages? You can do this. You can create additional templates for more granular control over your site appearance.

Click the **Add New** button top right to see the range of additional templates you can create.

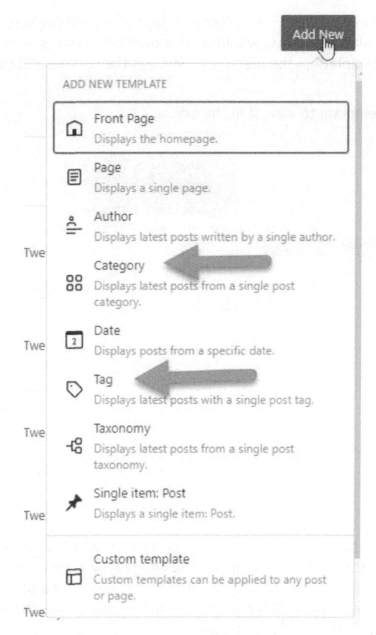

The **Custom template** at the bottom gives you ultimate control of your design, allowing you to create a unique template that may only be used on a single post or page! I don't recommend it, but you could create a different template for every page on your site.

Notice that you can create a template to be used specifically for category pages and another for tag pages.

When WordPress tries to render a category page, it will look for the category template first. If it finds that template, WordPress will use it. If it does not find that template, WordPress looks for the archive template (which is included in this theme).

WordPress templates are organized into this type of hierarchy. The hierarchy of templates that are considered when WordPress renders a page is beyond the scope of this introduction, but can you think what WordPress would do if it didn't find the archive template? It would look for the next template in the hierarchy, which is the one we edited earlier. The default **Home** template.

Click on the 404 template to view it in the editor.

You can see the header, footer, and the **Group** in the middle that shows the 404 message. At the top, the menu shows "404," and if you click on that, you can see the header and footer areas. If you go in and edit the header and footer areas as we did before, these changes will affect the whole site. If you edit the bit in the middle that shows the 404 message, that obviously only affects the 404 page display.

So why does editing the header or footer change this on all pages of the site?

The answer is that this theme has defined the header and footer as **Template Parts.** Template parts are self-contained designs, a lot like the reusable blocks we saw earlier in the book. This theme uses the same header and footer "template parts" in all templates that make up the theme. When you edit the header or footer, you are editing the template part, so changes are seen across all templates using these template parts.

You can see these **Template Parts** if you click on the WordPress logo in the top left to open the FSE sidebar.

Click the **Template Parts** menu.

You will see the following:

Template	Added by
Header	Twenty Twenty-Three
Footer	Twenty Twenty-Three
Comments	Twenty Twenty-Three
Post Meta	Twenty Twenty-Three

You can see the header and footer at the top. Click on the **Header**.

The header (that we modified) earlier is displayed. Open the **List View,** and you can see the blocks used.

This header was used in all templates for the Twenty Twenty-Three theme, so every page uses the same header. If we want to change the header on the site, we simply edit this template part, and those changes will be seen across the entire site.

But what if we wanted to use a different header on specific posts or pages on the site?

Simple. We can just create a new header and add it to the template that controls those posts or pages.

If you want to use a different header on category pages, just create the new header and then create (or edit) the category page template so that it uses the new header.

Let's add a custom header to the 404 page.

In the **Template Parts** screen, click the **Add New** button and enter the following:

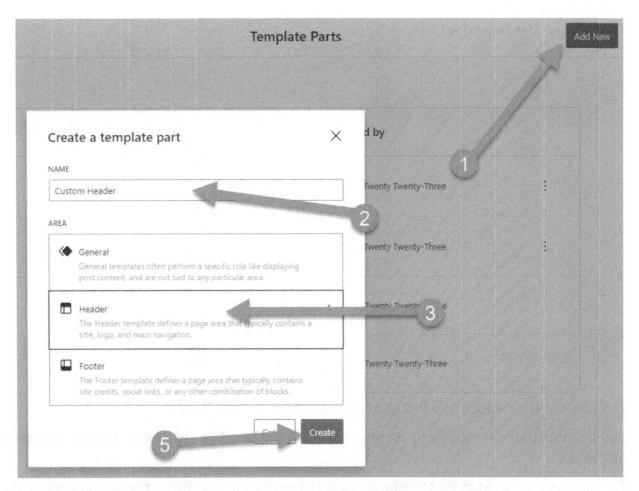

When you click the **Create** button, a new header template is created.

Open it and add a Site Title block to the header (/site). In the **Block Properties** panel on the right (cog button), change the typography to make this larger.

Save your header.

Now open the FSE editor sidebar by clicking the WordPress logo top left. On the **Template Parts** screen, you'll see your new "Custom Header."

Now click on **Templates** and select the 404 template.

Open the **List View** and delete the **Header** section using its **Options** menu.

Open the block inserter (+) and search for **Template Part**. Select it to add a template part block to your template:

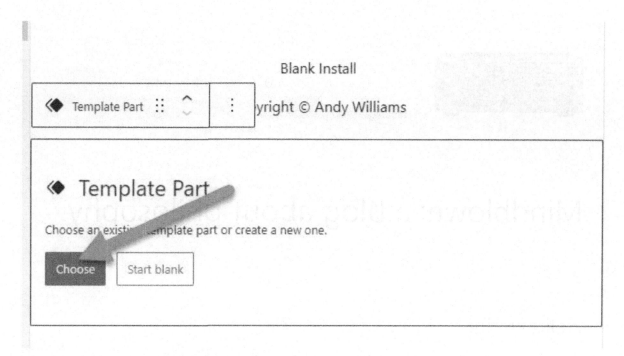

Click **Choose,** and you'll see your newly designed header:

Existing template parts

Click on it to select.

Now open the **List View** and drag the template part to the top.

Save your 404 template.

Now go and visit your site.

All the pages except the 404 page use the original header (as defined by those templates).

Mindblown: a blog about philosophy.

Hello world!

Welcome to WordPress. This is your first post. Edit
or delete it, then start writing!

January 12, 2023

In the address bar of your browser, after the domain name, add some random characters that will simulate a user going to a page that does not exist.

e.g., https://mydomain.com/fgskfdjg

This will load the 404 error page, which uses your new header:

Blank Install

404

This page could not be found.

Search...	🔎

Congratulations, you have used the full site editor to take control of your WordPress theme.

Where to Go from Here?

We've covered a lot of ground in this book. You should now be confident in finding your way around the WordPress Dashboard.

You have installed WordPress, installed the essential plugins, and configured everything so that your site is now ready for content.

So, what's the next step?

Create impressive content!

Create content, publish & repeat.

I have a couple of resources you may find useful.

YouTube Channel

Lots of video tutorials on using WordPress.

https://ezseonews.com/yt

O.M.G. Facebook Group

A group I initially created for my course students, but I welcome book readers too! Meet, chat, and discuss with other WordPress users. This is an ad-free zone, so you won't be bombarded with people trying to sell you stuff. You will be asked where you heard about the group when you click to join, so just say you are a reader of the book.

https://ezseonews.com/omg

My Site / Newsletter

Find lots of WordPress tutorials. You can sign up for my newsletter while you are there to get notified of new tutorials, books, courses, etc.

https://ezseonews.com/

Useful Resources

There are a few places that I would recommend you visit for more information.

WordPress Tutorials on my Website

https://ezseonews.com/category/wordpress/

My Other Webmaster Books

All my books are available as Kindle books and paperbacks. You can view them all here:

https://amazon.com/author/drandrewwilliams

I'll leave you to explore those if you are interested. You'll find books on various aspects of being a webmaster, such as creating high-quality content, SEO, CSS, etc.

My Video Courses

I have a growing number of video courses hosted on Udemy. You can view a complete list of these at my site:

https://ezseonews.com/udemy

There are courses on the same kinds of topics that my books cover, so SEO, Content Creation, WordPress, Website Analytics, etc.

Google Webmaster Guidelines

https://ezseonews.com/wmg - This is the webmaster's bible of what is acceptable and what is not in the eyes of the world's biggest search engine.

Google Analytics

http://www.google.com/analytics/ - The best free analytics program out there. When you have some free time to learn how to use Google Analytics, I recommend you upgrade from Get Clicky.

Please Leave a Review/Thought on Amazon

If you enjoyed this book, or even if you didn't, I'd love to hear your comments about it. You can leave your thoughts on the Amazon website.

Made in the USA
Las Vegas, NV
13 November 2023

80788090R00122